IF YOU LISTEN TO ME

Anti-Bullying Training for Acute Care Hospital Staff

DR. PHYLLIS BROWNING

Browning & Associates

CONTENTS

Ebook ISBN13: 978-1-7326818-0-4
Ebook ISBN10: 1-7326818-0-5

Print ISBN13: 978-1-7326818-1-1
Print ISBN10: 1-7326818-1-3

This book was previously titled *Nurse Bullying, Training in Acute Care Hospital
Settings: An Exploratory Study* (ISBN 978-0-692-92843-1), published in 2016.
Although published with a different title, this book is a second edition of the
original work.

PREFACE

In her book, *If You Listen to Me*, Dr. Phyllis Browning's goal is to change attitudes about workplace bullying by raising awareness of this harmful behavior. Readers will learn how to recognize and understand bullying and how to implement FIRE (Fear, Intimidation, Retaliation, Everyone) Training. FIRE is a robust training tool that can assist in alleviating bullying.

Although *If You Listen to Me* is primarily intended for leaders in the health care field, it will allow readers of all backgrounds to understand the motivation behind bullying and it effect on victims. Also, the evidence-based strategies and tools provided within this book can be adapted to improve any workplace environment.

ABSTRACT

Registered nurses have highly responsible and stressful jobs, which are often made much harder by workplace bullying. Inappropriate workplace behaviors can undermine their self-confidence in their ability to care for their patients, as well as cause stress. This not only adversely affects the health and wellbeing of nurses targeted by such acts, but also disrupts workflow, potentially jeopardizing patient safety.

This qualitative exploratory study explored nurses' perceptions regarding the effectiveness of currently offered training aimed at eradicating bullying, as well as improving their ability to cope with bullying. Their suggestions for improvements could assist in preventing bullying within their units.

Nurses' perceptions regarding the impact of bullying on patient safety and their ability to do their jobs were also explored. To delve into nurses' experiences, 14 registered nurses from the Oklahoma City area were purposively selected to take part in individual semi-structured telephone interviews that were recorded and transcribed for subsequent thematic analysis.

Analysis of participants' responses revealed themes that were common to the majority of the interviewees. The commonalities discovered were:

- Ineffectiveness of workplace anti-bullying training,
- Coping strategies employed by nurses,
- Benefits of anti-bullying training received,
- Obstacles to bullying prevention,
- Workplace fear of bullying and
- Anti-Bullying leadership training

These commonalities could assist nursing leaders in developing more effective training programs and creating a healthier work environment in which all nurses feel valued and supported.

DEDICATION

I dedicate this book, If You Listen to Me, to all the registered nurses who have experienced or witnessed bullying and may have suffered from its physical and emotion effects.

To my father, Jerrold Browning, and mother, Pamela Byrd-Walker. I am so proud to dedicate my book to you because I would not be the person I am today without your unceasing love and encouragement. You have supported me spiritually, financially, and emotionally, and have been there for me from the beginning. You inspired and motivated me to aim for goals that did not always seem attainable. You also taught me that we value much more those achievements that push us to work the hardest. Thank you for believing in me and giving me courage to persist, because there were times when I wanted to give up.

To my children, Ronnie and Haley, THANK YOU! Although you may not have contributed financially and academically to this project, your patience, love and support were invaluable. Ronnie, thank you for being so understanding, responsible and for dedicating countless hours of your time to care for your sister Haley in order to lessen my workload. You are both a great blessing in my life and I love you with all my heart.

ACKNOWLEDGMENTS

Thank you, God, for blessing me with health, mental strength, wisdom and perseverance, without which I would not be able to achieve my goal. Throughout my life, I followed your guidance and honored my father and mother. This first commandment gave me the strength and confidence to reach for my goals, while always being mindful of the love and guidance of my parents.

I would like to express my sincere gratitude to Dr. Randall Thompson for the constant support, unwavering dedication and insightful advice. I truly appreciate your mentorship and the countless hours you spent reviewing my work, helping me to become a better researcher and writer.

My warmest thanks also go to my committee members. I appreciate your patience, understanding and ongoing support throughout this process. Team THANK YOU!

INTRODUCTION

Nursing is one of the most stressful and challenging occupations because of the complex nature of health care, long working hours, an excessive workload and unsupportive management.[1] Stress in the work place may lead to the development of disruptive behaviors among nursing staff.[2]

Ongoing incidents of disruptive behaviors have been reported at all levels of health care sectors and solutions have often been difficult to implement. For many years, nurses have accepted being belittled, teased, verbally abused, made the object of offensive behaviors, intimidated, threatened, sabotaged and bullied.[3]

In the second decade of the 21st century, workplace bullying remained an unresolved problem in health care organizations worldwide.[4,5] The underlying cause of bullying involves interpersonal conflict that affects the mental wellbeing of nurses,[6] generates stress[7,8] and may precipitate suicide.[9] Lieber[8] espoused that bullying is oppression characterized by repeated aggression directed toward other individuals through physical or verbal abuse.

After decades of research into the repercussions of bullying,

Fry[10] posited that administrators may have forgotten the impact of bullying on nurses, and may have contributed to a culture of tolerance for admonishment and unreported bullying incidents. The combination of management's lack of response to the bullying issues and nurse non-reporting of incidents were among the casualties of bullying; consequently, such occurrences limited the identification of solutions.[10]

The results of this study provide new knowledge that may assist in developing in-service programs and training practices that might help to mitigate the social cognitive and physical effects of nurse bullying. Bullying is a complex issue for which no single solution exists to ameliorate the behavior of workplace bullies.[11]

Cognitive factors, such as effective coping strategies, act as deterrents and protect people from being at risk of emotional state changes.[11] As noted by Skehan,[12] nurse leaders lack programs to help subordinates deal with bullying behaviors within health care organizations. The importance of providing nurses with training about coping with bullying is that it may offer strategies for handling difficult situations. Effective anti-bullying training programs may create a positive work environment and preventive measures that enhance the personal lives of nurses and improve patient safety.[12]

"Life is a fight, but not everyone is a fighter. Otherwise, bullies would be an endangered species."

— ANDREW VACHSS

CHAPTER ONE

BACKGROUND

$\mathcal{B}$ullying contributes to absenteeism, low morale and decreased productivity among nurses.[13] Idsoe, Dyregrov and Idsoe[14] espoused that bullying is an interpersonal conflict that negatively affects the social-cognitive state of individuals. Bullying can trigger destructive reactions such as negative thoughts, alcohol and drug abuse, low mood and violent acts that may affect victims' personal and professional lives.[3,15]

From an organizational perspective, bullying is associated with social-cognitive stressors, burnout and workplace turnover. Workplace bullying may be avoided if nurses are prepared to respond appropriately, but lack of training can become an organizational impediment.[10]

Registered nurses (RNs) who are unable to manage stress are at risk of leaving the specialty or the profession entirely.[16] To reduce the negative effects on social cognitive state among nurses, an exploration of workplace anti-bullying training is imperative according to Hildebrandt.[17] Employees have had trouble identifying a common strategy to ascertain events that trigger bullying in the health care field. Abrahamson, Anderson, Anderson, Suitor and Pillemer[18] stated that nurses' perceptions of interpersonal conflict are strong triggers for burnout and turnover.

ॐ

STATEMENT OF THE PROBLEM

The dynamics within the health care culture and the highly stressful nature of patient care may contribute to a unique atmosphere of bullying.[19] Negative social interactions in the nursing profession affect the nursing shortage through increased turnover, mental and physical issues, hostile work environments and financial costs.[20] Workplace bullying in health care facilities damages the reputation of organizations and increases expenses.[8] Hutchinson and Hurley[21] suggested that repeated exposure to bullying behaviors affects employees' wellbeing, diminishes positive outcomes for patients, generates work-related stress and increases staff turnover.

The general problem is that bullying in the health care profession can cause increased stress for many persons and employee turnover.[22,23,24] Health care systems may have neglected to address bullying acts despite nurses possibly having experienced bullying in the workplace.[25] Bullying may be avoidable if nurses are prepared to respond to bullying behaviors appropriately through workplace training programs.[25] The lack of effective adaptive coping mechanisms stemming from an absence of appropriate training results in social dysfunction.[25]

The specific problem is that nurses are not adequately trained how to respond to and cope with workplace bullying. The inability of nurses to cope with bullying may impact their ability to do their jobs and possibly jeopardize patient safety.[26]

PURPOSE OF THE STUDY

The purpose of this qualitative study was to explore workplace training that nurses receive regarding bullying, nurses' perceptions regarding the effectiveness of that training, their ability to cope with bullying and to suggested areas for improved training. In addition, nurses' perceptions regarding how bullying impacts patient safety and the ability to do their jobs was explored.

The population for this study was RNs practicing in Oklahoma City metropolitan area hospitals. With more than 2.6 million nursing professionals in the United States, RNs are the largest nursing profession. Many will experience interpersonal conflict and would benefit from a training program that focuses on helping nurses to cope with bullying acts.[26] Nearly 58% of RNs work in an acute care setting. The lack of developed coping strategies to combat bullying tactics may potentially compromise patient safety.[26a]

SIGNIFICANCE OF THE STUDY TO LEADERSHIP

Leaders, such as nurses, physicians, administrators and educators serve as role models for followers. The role of leaders is to inspire and motivate followers. Wren[192] stated that relationship gaps in leadership often result from a lack of attention and communication between leaders and followers.

As recipients of bullying report complaints of verbal abuse and humiliation, targets of repeated aggression require serious attention from nurse leaders.[8] Inattention to complaints about unreasonable behavior perpetuates the problem of nurses being bullied, resulting in low productivity, stress and burnout.

Leaders have an obligation to ensure that the work environment provides a balance of healthy work and life that promotes a non-bullying tolerance culture and productive team.[27,28,29] Nurse management faces the challenge of finding an effective approach to mitigate bullying while advocating patient safety and competent care. This can only be achieved through development of workplace leadership skills and interpersonal relationships with and among the staff, to deter bullying behaviors.[21,30]

Individual coping strategies and training regarding ways to create solutions to change the culture that helps motivate and modify behaviors that are construed as bullying may be an alternative option.[31] Increased awareness of the effectiveness of workplace anti-bullying training and the ability to cope with bullying may lead health care administrators to promote a nurturing and zero-tolerance work environment.

NATURE OF THE STUDY

Qualitative methods facilitate investigations of existing problems through personal narratives; the use of scholarly research can foster practical interventions and improve employees' job performance.[32] The qualitative method allowed for gathering in-depth insight of nurses' perceptions of anti-bullying training programs.

Inclusion criteria for study participants were RNs employed in acute care inpatient hospital settings. Potential participants were selected from an Oklahoma Board of Nursing purchased list. After screening the purchased list, every eligible participant was assigned a number (e.g., 1-150) and placed into a random number generator that selected numbers and placed them into five 30-count columns.

Each number generated was matched to the first 150 participants' assigned numbers and each participant selected received an invitation letter to participate in telephone interviews. The letter provided an explanation of the study and directions for returning an ink-signed informed consent letter via email, fax or mail. Interested participants were asked to respond by phone or email with their contact information and afterwards, a short telephone screening interview was conducted to verify eligibility to participate.

Qualitative research is an effective method to gain insight into health care professionals' thoughts and feelings on an issue.[33] Peter[34] emphasized that the qualitative approach is an appropriate method to discern the sensitivity of a topic like an individual's emotional state. Qualitative research is appropriate when the goal is to understand participants' perceptions or experiences using one of five designs: Ethnography, grounded theory, phenomenology, narrative or case study.[35]

Qualitative methods are appropriate when limited research exists about a topic of interest.[35] In qualitative research, the method requires a researcher to actively engage with participants during every step to provide meaningful insights that can be used to bring significant changes in dealing with an issue or problem.[187]

Qualitative methods make it possible to understand individuals' realities in a natural setting or in a social context using multiple data sources.[35] Campbell[35] emphasized that the focus of qualitative exploratory inquiry study design is on experiences and perceptions of reality to help researchers understand the participants' actions in different scenarios.

Qualitative investigators attempt to understand and interpret a complex phenomenon in the narratives of individuals within the context of their natural setting.[36] One advantage of qualitative methods is that the researcher becomes an instrument in the study. According to Leedy and Ormrod,[37] researchers acknowledge the fact that thoughts and actions impact the outcomes, meanings, experiences and perceptions under study.

As described by Leedy and Ormrod,[37] quantitative methods do not allow investigators to participate in the study but to act only as observers. As expressed by Leedy and Ormrod[37], the quantitative approach does not permit the development of the personal connection needed to draw out the emotions, thoughts and meanings of participants as in a qualitative study.

Qualitative methods do not involve identifying a potential causal relationship between variables but rather, the focus is on how respondents perceive experiences of the phenomenon under study.[38,39] To understand situations that contribute to nurse bullying, the use of a qualitative exploratory inquiry approach allowed for exploring participants' social-cognitive insights into workplace bullying.

The qualitative approach was appropriate for this study to seek answers to open-ended questions from a small number of participants to produce valuable, holistic knowledge of registered nurses' perceptions of the perceived influence of anti-bullying in-service training.

RESEARCH QUESTIONS

Wolf et al.[40] stated that a beneficial study begins with well-developed research questions. The following research questions (RQs) guided the study:

RQ1: How have work place training programs influenced the ability, or inability, of RNs to respond to bullying in inpatient hospital settings?

RQ2: What is the perceived influence on job performance in inpatient hospital settings of workplace training on bullying?

RQ3: What is the perceived influence on patient safety of workplace training on bullying in inpatient hospital settings?

RQ4: What do RNs perceive that inpatient hospitals can do to improve workplace training on bullying?

&

CONCEPTUAL FRAMEWORK

The level of violence in the health care field is a widespread humanitarian concern and problem.[41,42] Workplace bullying is a significant concern for nurses and nurse leaders that has led to social-cognitive problems and unhealthy work environments.[7,6] Despite documentation of the emotional effects of bullying, little is known about the training needs for nurses working in high stress areas.[43]

Understanding the relationship between an individual's perceptions and conceptions is important for nurses and nurse leaders. Such understanding raises awareness of interpretations of nurse perceptions of working conditions, interpersonal phenomena and the shifting balance of work and personal lives. Researchers use system theory to understand the complex dynamic of human relationships and social culture changes.[44]

System theory is a framework inquiry for multifaceted situations that requires a comprehensive approach to the solution rather than information gathered of a specific phenomenon.[44] A general system theory is selected to understand normative viewpoints on workplace training about bullying behaviors that have presented challenges to the hospital system. The system of focus in this dissertation study was on RNs in the hospital setting.

Von Bertalanffy's[45] General System Theory (GST) is an important construct in the social and behavioral sciences. A system is defined by Laszlo and Krippner[44] as "a group of interacting components that conserves some identifiable set of relations with the sum of the components plus their relations (i.e., the system itself) conserving some identifiable set of relations to other entities (including other systems)."

According to Laszlo and Krippner,[44] the GST approach is based on the belief that the researcher should have specific and intimate knowledge of smaller items rather than general and abstract knowledge of larger items. The knowledge encourages the development of a well-defined study based on individualism and life experiences. The application of system theory provides a framework for holistic exploration of complex phenomena, events and experiences of interpersonal, intergroup and human interaction without changing individual's reality or experience.

GST was developed to incorporate constructs or components: A component has an effect on the functioning of the whole, and each component is affected by a least one other component in the system. Hospital is a system operating within the broader environment, which affects the quality of a nurse's workplace, imposing certain expectations regarding staff conduct. Each nurse's behavior and perception intertwines with other personnel and affects the system (i.e., work environment).

DEFINITION OF TERMS

The following definitions of terms provide a basic understanding of key words used in the study.

Hospital acute care settings include cardiac, medical, surgical and labor and delivery.[184]

Bullying is unwelcome, inappropriate conduct against individuals to gain control or harm individuals. Bullying refers to aggressive, belittled, teased, verbally abused, intimidated, threatened or sabotaged.[46,7,47,48]

Workplace bullying involves repeated abusive and intimidating acts, disrespect, humiliation or social isolation imposed by someone at the workplace that affects an individual's work performance or personal lives.[70]

Patient safety is achieved through the prevention of errors and adverse effects to patients associated with health care provided by medical staff, aiming to increase positive outcomes.[49]

&

ASSUMPTIONS

According to Van Manen,[50] all research includes factors like assumptions and bias that are beyond a researcher's control. Leedy and Ormrod[37] explained that "assumptions are so basic that, without them, the research problem itself could not exist." The following assumptions are acknowledged for this qualitative explorative inquiry study:

- Participants were forthcoming and willing to participate in the study.
- Participants were truthful in their responses to the interview questions.
- All participants were asked about their experience of workplace bullying in an acute care unit.

According to DeVeaux, Velleman and Bock[51] a researcher's knowledge and presence as an instrument in the study creates potential biases. The researcher as an instrument could influence the participants' perceptions, responses or decisions to participate.

SCOPE OF THE STUDY

A projected sample of RNs was recruited through a purchased list obtained from the Oklahoma Board of Nursing (OBN).[168] Qualitative research has no clear guidelines on how small or large the sample size may be. According to Merriam,[39] the sample size should be appropriate to attain credibility and accuracy, to understand the phenomenon to be studied and to generate saturation. The standard sample size for a qualitative research study is 6-12 participants according to Langdride[52] and Moustakas'[53] suggestion of 12-15.

The exact number of participants cannot be determined until no new insights, ideas or concepts are obtained (i.e., data saturation) from interviews. Upon analyzing the collected data, saturation occurred at 12 interviews. Nonetheless, to confirm that data saturation had been achieved, two additional interviews were conducted. Information gained from 14 telephone-based interviews with the study participants formed the dataset that was subjected to a comprehensive thematic analysis.

The participants were asked nine open-ended questions to gather a detailed narrative of nurses' perspectives about workplace bullying and in-service training needs. Participants' responses were analyzed and coded to identify themes, patterns and relationships.

LIMITATIONS

Limitations to this qualitative exploratory inquiry study included my previous knowledge, experience and ability to interpret the participants' responses without bias. Because of the sensitive nature of the study, another potential limitation may have been the participants' purposeful distortion of an experience because of the fear of reliving the event.

The experiences of nurses participating in the study impede transferability to another nursing population or demonstrate that the participants were representative of all nurses. Participants from other nursing settings and in different geographic locations may have other types of experiences or interpretations of workplace bullying.

Using telephone interviews to collect data did not allow for observation of participants' body language or facial expressions, which represents a limitation. The advantage of using telephone interviews is that the data collection method provides a non-threatening environment for participants as they share insightful and often sensitive information with the interviewer.

Recalling traumatic events such as workplace bullying experiences could re-trigger emotional responses from participants. A participant's strong emotion could influence results because of personal experience, which represents an additional limitation. No participants expressed any emotional distress during the individual telephone interviews.

DELIMITATIONS

The primary step in establishing delimitations of a study is the selection of the problem to be addressed.[54] This dissertation study consisted of registered nurses in the Oklahoma City, Oklahoma area whose contact information existed on a list purchased from the OBN. The OBN provided a list of potential participants that included employment setting, job title, patient population served, clinical specialty (when applicable), home address and licensure status. Participants were delimited to direct caregivers to patients in hospital settings.

The study was delimited to RNs who worked in a hospital setting, held an RN license and lived in Oklahoma. Simon and Goes[54] stated that interview questions and methods are a means of delimiting a study. The interview questions were open-ended but focused on the phenomenon selected as the research problem to delimit the study. The entire research process occurred within a period of 16 weeks.

CHAPTER ONE SUMMARY

Chapter One included a description of various perspectives regarding the major causes and consequences of bullying in the health care field. Nurses have been scrutinized and accused of bullying behaviors toward other acute care nurses.[55] A need exists for an exploration of nurses' experiences with bullying and the consequences of workplace violence on their personal and professional lives in order to improve their coping strategies and improve patient care.[56,57]

The rationale for exploring anti-bullying training is to add to the body of nursing knowledge about bullying, create a better understanding of the benefits and shortcomings of anti-bullying training and help leaders to develop new training programs on anti-bullying for nurses.

Chapter Two contains a review of the literature about the history of workplace bullying and RNs' perspectives on workplace training, coping strategies and patient safety.

Chapter One Notes

CHAPTER TWO

REVIEW OF THE LITERATURE

*B*ased on the literature review, health care organizations do not have a clear, effective and consistent method for the development or implementation of bullying prevention strategies. Victims, leaders and organizations are at a loss how to address and cope with bullying among colleagues. Although the development of prevention programs is complicated, the lack of consistency will continue to be problematic.

The intent of this study was to explore current training programs offered, if any, based upon participants' beliefs and to offer recommendations for improvement. No study could be found in the literature on the perceptions of RNs' anti-bullying training programs in acute inpatient hospital settings.

HISTORICAL OVERVIEW OF WORKPLACE BULLYING

European scholars were the first to emerge with concerns and the need to understand the rights of workers in relation to workplace problems.[58],[59],[60] Leymann,[58] a Swedish psychologist, studied hostile behaviors in the workplace and referred to mobbing as a type of interpersonal conflict that encroaches upon victims' civil rights. The first attempt to address bullying in the workforce occurred in the 1980s.[61] The research into bullying began with researchers identifying and defining the pervasive pattern of bullying. Researcher themes include repeated and ongoing attacks, aggression-based differences, self-importance and lack of empathy.[63]

Four critical incident phases of mobbing in the workplace identified by Leymann[58] were as follows:

- Phase 1, the original critical incident, involves observing employees for triggering states in the workplace;
- Phase 2, mobbing and stigmatizing, begins at the point of manipulation of an event over long periods of injurious behavior to "get at a person" or punish the person. Manipulation from the bully can result in damage to the victim's reputation, often leading to the victim's social self-isolation due to the perceived threat of violence.
- In Phase 3, personnel administration acknowledges that management is aware of the problem and confronts an individual that had violated justice. Leymann[58] stated that poor management and problem-solving skills was a system factor that often leads to workplace aggression occurrences and results in experiencing post-traumatic stress.
- Phase 4, expulsion, is the most dangerous phase: During

this phase victims suffer from physical, social and psychosomatic effects.

Workplace bullying is a broad term that represents a diverse range of behaviors. The most common characteristics of workplace bullying described in the literature are mobbing, violence, workplace harassment, hostile work environments, abusive behaviors, horizontal violence, hostility and labeling as an oppressed group.[64] Bullying can involve physical harassment that can result in death, isolation and extortion.[63] Workplace bullying can be disastrous to employers and may violate the human rights of employees in the United States.[185]

Bullying is a subset of prohibited civil rights acts that overlap with discriminatory harassment acts that include those involving race, national origin, color, sex, age, disability, sexual orientation or religion.[65] When employers fail to respond appropriately, civil rights acts may sanction legal action to protect individuals from bullying. No administrative, federal or states' laws address workplace bullying.[66] The inadequate protection for employees inspired David Yamanda, Professor of Law and founding Director of the New Workplace Institute at Suffolk University Law School in Boston, to author an anti-bullying model legislation called the Healthy Workplace Bill.[170] The Healthy Workplace Bill[170] is intended to offer employee resolutions, assist in employee advocacy, set policies regarding bullying and ingrain a standard of conduct that establishes zero-tolerance for workplace bullying.

Bullying is a multicultural and multi-organizational phenomenon. The common problem is that many individuals describe bullying in various terms and overlook the seriousness of the consequences.[174] In a survey of students from 52 countries regarding the definition of workplace bullying, Saunders, Huynh, and Goodman-Delahunty[175] reported that 93% of the participants defined bullying differently. Ninety-three percent of the participants believed that, in order to be classified as having been bullied, individuals must have experienced negative behaviors, and 86.3% believed that individuals must have experienced physical hurt or harm. Of the 1,095 participants, 25% reported that bullying was unprofessional conduct that violates workers' rights and hinders individuals from performing job duties effectively.

Personal experiences of bullying lead people to formulate a view about what is considered bullying, when aggressive acts are intentional or negative behavior is harmful. Recognizing and understanding individuals' perceptions is crucial to meeting the safety, protection and education needed so that effective coping strategies are suitable for individuals at the workplace.

Research by Cleary, Hunt, Walter and Robertson,[108] Rhodes et al.[22] and Thobaben[13] supported the acknowledgement that bullying denies individuals' basic human rights, dignity and freedom. Bullying actions not only result in negative consequences but are the core of the violation of peoples' civil rights. Because peoples' civil rights are violated in a location that is perceived as a safe place, people are left feeling defenseless. Workplace bullying undermines the right to work with dignity.

PERSPECTIVES ON WORKPLACE BULLYING

The United States workplace bullying initiative began with anti-bullying activist, David Yamada, an attorney who was among the first to lobby for adequate legal workplace anti-bullying laws in the United States since 2000.[70] The inadequacy of an existing workplace anti-bullying act delays the use of punitive actions, escalates bullying behaviors and reduces incentives for employers.[65] In 2012, Davidson and Harrington[66] reported that the Healthy Workplace Bill[170] was recognized by 28 states and "[there was] no clear-cut legal remedy for victims of workplace bullying in place in the United States." American workers can use federal and state laws associated with the Civil Rights Act, which defines bullying as discrimination or abusive behaviors.[67]

Martin and LaVan[68] conducted a review of the literature and examined a random sample of 45 United States litigated cases from 2003–2007 using policy-capturing methodology. The results revealed that the bases for the legal considerations were as follows: 35.6% Title VII race discrimination, 28.9% gender discrimination, 6.7% national origin discrimination, and 2.2% religious discrimination.[68] One out of 20 cases was identified as intentional infliction of emotional distress.

Workplace bullying was on the increase in the first decade of the 21st century in the human service workforce in the United States.[69] Forty-seven percent of Americans have experienced workplace bullying or witnessed the behavior.[70] Workplace Bullying Institute[70] documented that 54 million American workers experience workplace abusive behaviors every year, either as a victim or bystander. Workplace bullying has been a common problem not only in the United States but also in other countries.[71] Scholars have conducted a wide range of research on bullying in the nursing profession in countries other than the United States, predominantly in Europe, Japan, the Philippines and Australia.[46,7,47,48,72]

A qualitative descriptive study by Simons and Mawn[71] explored new registered nurses' responses to nurse-nurse bullying incidents in Massachusetts from the original survey in 2008. Seventy-one percent of new graduate registered nurses were employed in a hospital setting and 12% worked in long-term care. Out of 511 surveys sent, 184 (36%) completed the survey with narrative response. Of the completed surveys, 139 respondents shared their experiences of workplace bullying, 14 claimed to have been witnesses to bullying, and the remaining participants submitted non workplace-related bullying that was not included in the results.

Simons and Mawn[71] acknowledged that one limitation was that 184 nurses could not be used to represent all participants in the study. The results identified four factors that clarified the evidence of workplace bullying and described the novice nurses' experiences: "structural bullying, nurses [*eating their young*], feeling out of the clique and leaving the job." Simons and Mawn[71] explained that *eating their young* was described as "extreme hostility" experienced within the first year of employment by one participant. The expression "nurses eating their young" refers to veteran nurses bullying younger or novice nurses. Additionally, 38 nurses reported that they had experienced negative behaviors during the orientation phase of employment, and others shared similar stories of working with unhappy nurses and being afraid to ask questions because of their fear of retaliation.

Simons and Mawn[71] indicated that structural bullying experienced by nurse participants occurred when being subjected to unfair actions (scheduling demands and unmanageable workloads) by supervisors. One older nurse working in the long-term care setting experienced social isolation and complained of a lack of teamwork, as well as the prevalence of cliques and sarcasm. A general consensus among the novices who considered resignation was that workplace bullying was the main reason behind their decision to leave. Similarly, Ali,[73] Broome and Williams-Evans[3] and Baker[74] described *eating their young* as nurse bullying behaviors that produce a toxic working and personal environment among nursing staff, especially among novice health care organizations and nursing schools.

Berry et al.[46] conducted an exploratory, descriptive cross-sectional Internet-based survey with 190 novice registered nurses to determine the prevalence and effects of workplace bullying on productivity. The participants were recruited from Ohio and Indiana; 91.4% were female and 8.6% were male who had worked in health care facilities for less than two years (i.e., novice nurses). The results revealed that 63% of novice nurses experienced bullying by a colleague, with 72.6% reporting that the bullying incidents occurred within a month prior to the study, and 21.3% stated that they had encountered bullying acts daily for three months. During a 6-month period 44.7% reported recurring events in which they were targets, 55.3% reported no experiences with workplace bullying and 77% reported being repeated targets of bullying that impacted their productivity. The study results revealed that workplace bullying is problematic for health care organizations and results in new nurses lacking effective communication practices, coping skills and commitment, leading to decreased productivity.

According to Indvik and Johnson,[75] an estimated 25% of bullied workers and 20% of witnesses resign as a result of bullying. In the United States the average workplace expense associated with voluntary termination among nurses may range between $4.9 and $43.4 billion annually.[42] Workplace bullying is a complex problem that has economic, stakeholder and legal ramifications for patient care organizations.[75]

The stereotype for nurses includes subservience to doctors which has led to violent acts, workplace stress and doctor-nurse oppression.[76,77] In 2012 Farrell and Shafiei[78] conducted a study in Australia on workplace aggression among nurses and midwives. Five thousand questionnaires were distributed and 1,495 returned, representing a 30% response rate. The results indicated that 52% of the participants experienced workplace aggression on the job; 32% of 52% reported that they were mostly bullied by co-workers or management. Following the bullying experiences, 83% of the participants reported the belief that the perpetrator's personality contributed significantly to bullying incidents.

In 2010 MacIntosh, Wuest, Gray and Cronkhite[62] studied 21 women from various occupations (i.e., social workers, registered nurses, licensed nurse practitioners, housekeepers, therapists, home care workers and nurse educators) to examine perspectives about work after being bullied on the job. Twenty of the participants reported that their perception of work had changed because of their experience with bullying and that they were conflicted in their ethics, values and expectations. Study findings included evidence of a decrease in care quality and job satisfaction among the participants. Workplace bullying has serious consequences for individuals and organizations including employee turnover, decreased productivity, psychosocial hazards and emotional and physical health problems.[79]

Lieber[8] stated that of 170 human resource professionals from the web-based provider Workplace Answer, Inc., who reported having been bullied, 45% experienced stress-related physiological problems such as insomnia, anxiety, digestive problems and lifestyle issues (financial problems, hopelessness, fear, absenteeism or a desire to resign) as a result of bullying. In the same study, 40% of the participants never reported the incident of bullying, 3% of the participants sued their employer for unlawful harassment (e.g., workplace bullying), and 4% reported the bullying experienced to federal or state agencies.

Lieber[8] documented that common excuses mangers gave to avoid addressing the behaviors included that the individual perpetrating the bullying was a long-term employee and that the behavior was simply an aspect of the bully's personality. Berry et al.[46] suggested that until leaders eliminate bullying through effective policies and training, workplace bullying will remain a serious concern. Viollis[45] stated, "The vast majority of incidents of workplace violence are completely preventable if employees know what to look for and how to report it." Longo[6] stated that if health care organizations included bullying as a part of an in-house code of conduct policy, employees may be encouraged to report bullying acts and leaders would be obligated to enforce the rules.

CULTURAL INFLUENCES ON BULLYING

Ariza-Montes et al.[79] gathered data with the Fifth European Working Conditions Survey in 2010. Data obtained from 43,000 individuals who participated in interviews indicated that the bullying incidence rate among health care workers was 11.3%, with 38% reporting psychological harassment in the United States, and 44% of nurses experienced some form of bullying during their tenure. Regardless of the origin of bullying, workplace bullying among health care workers is more common than in any other profession.[79]

Common workplace bullying triggers include:

- Individual and personal differences,
- Characteristics of the setting in which the incident occurs (e.g., long-term, acute care),
- Prevalence of young women (25-39) among the staff and
- Disparity in educational levels.

Alarming concerns are that young women experience bullying more often than other individuals, and that special attention is needed for this group who feel displeased with their current work environment.[79] Out of 43,000 participants, 385 Canadian nurses who claimed to be victims of bullying reported more burnout, less job satisfaction and more psychological stress than other nurses who did not label themselves as bully victims.[79]

Samnani and Singh[80] conducted a 20-year literature review focused on the consequences of workplace bullying and found that culture could be a precursor to workplace bullying. In one instance, power distance (i.e., cultural perceptions of employer-employee relations in the workplace) played a role in determining how countries respond to workplace bullying. The perception of bullying is dependent on the different culture perspective of acceptance of power distance.

Power distance is defined as people in high positions who believe that power is unequally distributed within an organization and differs between individuals; whereas, low power cultures expect that power is shared equally. Countries with higher power distance are likely to have many perpetrators and are less likely to punish them for bullying behaviors, which increases the number of incidents. Employees living in a power distance society are accepting of the hierarchical societies unfair treatment. As a result, individuals experiencing bullying actions often respond negatively. At the employee level, cultural values influence bullying actions and negative reactions. Samnani and Singh[80] reported that personal (i.e., psychological and physical) consequences of bullying for employees increased during the 20-year period of the literature reviewed.

Workplace bullying occurs cross-culturally. Victims feel threatened and humiliated, and they experience physical and psychological harm.[81] In environments where bullying occurs, uncivil behaviors become acceptable.[82] In order to understand how culture significantly influences bullying, Power et al.[81] examined and compared the cultural differences in the acceptability of workplace bullying behaviors in 14 countries, especially focusing on work-related bullying (WRB) and physically intimidating bullying (PIB). WRB was defined as a delegation of unreasonable tasks and deadlines, and PIB was defined as behaviors such as shouting and anger. Respondents were from various countries including Argentina, Hong Kong, Africa, India, Taiwan and the United States.

Countries with a high performance orientation (e.g, Asia, Latin American, Africa, sub-Saharan Africa) are likely to accept bullying in the workforce as an acceptable trade off in the pursuit of workplace performance results.[81] All cultures maintain beliefs about acceptable employee behaviors and would welcome potential intervention, but differences in cultural acceptance of bullying in the workplace hamper efforts to establish global anti-bullying standards.[81] Workers in countries with strong humane orientation disapprove of workplace behavior that devalues others.[83] Although few studies have focused on the influence of language on the outcome of bullying, language is power and the instrument of culture[83]

Assertive cultures may accept harsh communication to subordinates whereas other cultures may find harsh communication offensive, disruptive, and rude. Vickers[84] stated that the manner of speaking in oppressive and aggressive cultures plays a role in triggering violent acts in employees. Individuals in countries with a humane orientation believe that bullying shows low respect toward human values and disrupts relationships between employees; reducing PIB and WRB improves quality of work life among employees.[84] Lack of justice and desensitization leads to the normalization and acceptance of violence in the organizational culture; violence becomes a cost rather than a human issue with safety, ethics and justice.[84] Desensitization and normalization of violence in organizations leads to the breakdown of an individual's internal restraints.[84]

Employees who observe that perpetrators are not being punished for their violence become tolerant or condone the violent behaviors.[84] When management is aware of bullying behaviors yet chooses to ignore the issue, the culture of bullying becomes acceptable.[13] The accumulated information from the literature indicates a lack of awareness of the significant effects of negative behaviors on individuals who are bullied.

SELF-LABELING VICTIMS

Employees who self-label themselves as victims of workplace bullying are more likely to become exposed to future bullying acts in the future.[57] Vie et al.[57] found that self-labeling is an important factor in the bullying-health relationship and acts as a negative circle of events that increases the amount of exposure and stress among victims. Self-labeling acts as a catalyst on the relationship between individuals exposed to bullying behaviors and their health, and significantly increases exposure to bullying and negative health outcomes when in a low bullying environment.[57] In a higher bullying acts environment, self-labeling makes no difference on individual health outcomes.[57]

One explanation for cyclical victim self-labeling is what Vie et al.[57] described as the cognitive theory of trauma that explains how victims acknowledge vulnerability and helplessness. Vie et al.[57] referred to the self-concept theory to explain the relationship between victims and the effects of bullying. When individuals adopt an identity as victims, they generate increases in potential stressors when bullied, decrease their coping abilities and generate more bullying events. Workplace bullying is a key occupational stressor and occupational health and safety concern.[13,57] A hospital environment in which staff nurses work includes high patient acuity and patients coping with terminal illness, extreme pain, death and loss, all of which contribute to a stressful workplace.[110]

Hecktman[111] stated that nurses are particularly at risk of job-related stressors. Nurses often overlook emotional experiences and are overwhelmed with responsibilities and may develop a poor perception of negative emotions, undue stress, feelings of powerlessness and poor coping strategies.[112,16] Nurses' emotional distress may foster a toxic work environment.[113] When nurses are working in a high stress area, they are at greater risk of depersonalization and jeopardizing patient safety.[114,25] Nurses frequently experience isolation, increased workload and job dissatisfaction.[115] Self-awareness helps nurses to take control over their emotions and transition out of self-victimization.[57]

Nurses who accept the victim stereotype may struggle to overcome that image and internalize powerlessness.[116] Repeated exposure to bullying validates employees' opinions of themselves as victims of workplace mistreatment. Self-labeling victims report more health complaints than non-self-labeling victims.[57] Self-labeling nurses report considerably lower job satisfaction, high burnout and serious mental and physical health consequences.[57]

A consensus among scholars postulates that bullying and violence in the workplace has increased despite the serious effects.[84] Nursing professionals have accepted bullying behaviors as part of the fundamental structure of the nursing profession, despite detrimental results.[13,84] According to Vickers[84] efficiency, economic rationalism and misrepresentation of justice-seeking responses hamper attempts at reducing bullying, violence in the workplace and negative health outcomes.

PHENOMENON OF POST-TRAUMATIC STRESS

According to the American Psychiatric Association (APA)[85] and the National Center for PTSD,[86] individuals who have encountered or observed a traumatic event (e.g., violent personal assaults, a serious accident or an event that is scary to see or hear about) may manifest a mental disorder called post-traumatic stress disorder (PTSD). PTSD affects 3.5% of the adult population in the United States, and 8.7% are at risk of PTSD.[85]

Adults with PTSD have symptoms long after experiencing a traumatic event, such as disturbing feelings and thoughts, numbing, hyper-arousal (aggression and self-destruction), flashbacks, nightmares, negative cognitions and moods (i.e., anger, intense fear, sadness, blaming self and others, estrangement from others), persistent avoidance and re-experienced helplessness and horror.[85,87,99,14,88,89,86,90]

PTSD as a medical diagnosis originated when veterans of the Vietnam War started complaining of reliving violence to which they had been exposed; however, PTSD symptoms can occur in persons who have undergone other traumatic situations such as mugging, torture and verbal or physical abuse.[91] According to the National Institute of Mental Health (NIMH),[91] victims are likely to show more aggression and violence towards others or may intentionally continue engaging in violent events (e.g., abuse), which seems to intensify their PTSD symptoms.

PTSD affects millions of people annually, and approximately 7.7 million adults are known to suffer from the disorder.[91] NIMH[91] reported that PTSD is a serious illness that requires medical attention. The initial onset of the disorder varies depending on the individual. Various researchers report that victims show signs of event flashbacks, thoughts of endangering self or others, bad dreams, avoidance of familiar places, insomnia and gastrointestinal (GI) disturbances.[87,88,90] Broome and Williams-Evans[3] noted that nurses develop psychological symptoms (e.g., PTSD, depression and low self-esteem) and physical changes (e.g., chest pain, headache, eating disorders and gastric discomfort) from traumatic events.

PTSD symptoms are the most commonly reported consequences following a work-related traumatic event.[92,93] Concerns among the nursing population include the fact many health care organizations have problems with nurses experiencing PTSD symptoms following work-related traumatic events.[94] PTSD is also an important safety concern among health care professionals, predominantly nurses.[95,93]

Intensive Care Unit (ICU) nurses have been shown to develop work-related PTSD symptoms after traumatic events.[96] To explore whether nurses suffer from PTSD as a direct association with traumatic events, Mealer, Jones and Moss[97,98] surveyed 744 ICU nurses who were members of the American Association of Critical Care Nurses (AACN) across the United States about the ICU work environment and the development of PTSD symptoms. Each participant completed the Post-traumatic Diagnostic Scale (PDS), an instrument to identify, diagnose and measure the symptoms of PTSD according the standards of the Diagnostic and Statistical Manual of Mental Disorders (DSM-IV).[97,98]

Mealer et al.[97,98] reported that 21% of the ICU nurses might be diagnosed with PTSD on the basis of the PDS, and that 70% of the ICU nurses experienced symptoms for a duration longer than three months while working in the ICU. The most commonly reported symptoms were anxiety (18%) and depression (11%); 80% of the participants reported feelings of exhaustion that changed their emotional state or self-care behaviors. Out of the 80% who reported feelings of exhaustion, 61% reported emotional exhaustion, 44% expressed depersonalization and 50% experienced a decline in personal accomplishment. The study results suggested that 8% of the ICU nurses who were highly resilient reported significantly lower symptoms of PTSD compared to 25% of less resilient nurses.

Czaja et al.[99] surveyed 173 pediatric acute care nurses to gain an understanding of the connection between working in a stressful environment and the risk of PTSD. The nurses worked in various departments (such as medical, surgical, oncology, pediatric intensive care and emergency room) at a tertiary-care childrens hospital in Denver, Colorado. Nurses were categorized into unit types described as high and low-intensity units. Fifty-six percent of the respondents worked in high-intensity units: Oncology, intensive care or emergency room. Among the respondents, 21% (n = 36) met the criteria for PTSD diagnosis, 91% (n = 31) reported having nightmares related to working conditions and 50% had considered a career change. Nurses who worked in a medical unit had a slightly higher occurrence of

PTSD symptoms. In general, nurses in all five units reported experiencing PTSD symptoms that lasted longer than three months.

PTSD symptoms are common complaints from nurses working in high-intensity units.[94] In a descriptive cross-sectional survey, Gillespie et al.[94] surveyed 208 workers from six hospital emergency rooms in the Midwestern region of the United States to analyze PTSD symptoms among emergency workers based on workplace aggression. Of the 208 participants, 86.5% were white and 71.2% were females. The study results indicated that 57% of the participants were at minimal risk for developing PTSD. The study results also revealed that 50–58% of nurses were exposed to verbal or physical aggression and had a higher risk of developing symptoms of PTSD, followed by 20–24% among physicians.

The proportion of nurses in need of care for PTSD has been a nationwide problem, illustrating the importance of the need for solutions in the health care sector.[100,101,102] PTSD is more prevalent among nurses than any other health problem.[103] The prevalence of work-related traumatic incidents and the consequences of PTSD have increased among hospital-based health care providers.[95]

Cavanaugh, Campbell and Messing[104] analyzed data from the Safe at Work Study to explore health and work consequences resulting from work-related violence among nurses and nursing personnel. A sample of 1,044 participants was recruited from three hospitals that included a geriatric care center. The participants completed an online or paper baseline assessment survey between May and September 2007. The Primary Care PTS screen was used to identify workers who had tested positive for PTS during a 6-month monitoring period. Women between the ages of 19 and 68, white and married (64.8%) reported having one or more work-related traumatic incidents at work that triggered PTSD. One-quarter of the intensive care nurses and one-fifth of surgery nurses reported experiencing PTSD or depression during the 6-month survey. Recurring exposure to work-related trauma has been linked to comorbid PTSD. PTSD contributes to nurses not being able to perform their occupational roles and engaging in counter-productive behaviors such as medication errors and interpersonal violence in hospitals.[104]

Rodríguez-Muñoz, Moreno-Jimenez, Sanz Vergel and Hernández[105] explored the prevalence of PTSD symptoms among victims of bullying. The purpose of the study was twofold:

- Assess the prevalence and intensity of post-traumatic stress disorder (PTSD) symptoms in victims of bullying and
- Explore whether victims of bullying differ in basic assumptions compared to a control group.

A sample of 183 victims of bullying and 183 control group participants from 10 different regions of Spain participated in the research. The results showed that 42.6% of the sample met all DSM-IV-TR criteria for PTSD whereas 54.1% did not fulfill the A1 criterion. The A1 criterion refers to "[a] person [who] experienced, witnessed or was confronted with an event or events that involved actual or threatened death or serious injury, or a threat to the physical integrity of self or others."

Post-traumatic symptoms were more prevalent among women (49%) than men (35.3%). Furthermore, victims showed significantly more negative beliefs about the world, other people and themselves than did non-bullied controls. The results fit well with the cognitive theory of trauma.

WORK-RELATED STRESS IN NURSING

In 2011, Rogers[106] estimated that 17 million workers were employed in the health care and social service sector. Registered nurses constituted approximately 2 million of the workers, and 70% of nurses worked in hospitals. Nursing is a stressful and often overwhelming profession.[107] The effects of bullying and cumulative work-related stressors (e.g., increase workload and job demands) can result in significant emotional disturbances.[107]

Results of a study conducted by Roberts, Scherer and Bowyer[117] suggested that workplace stressors may be known as a source of bullying. The purpose of the study was to examine job stress from two different approaches: Whether job stress escalates incivil behaviors and whether psychological capital prevents incivil responses to workplace stress.

A sample of 390 working adults (36% male and 64% female) from various industries, who had been employed between 6 months and 2 years, participated in the study. The participants, who ranged in age from 19 to 52, were recruited from two online research applications: SONA and SocialPsychology.org from a Midwestern university.

The results presented by Roberts et al.[117] showed a positive relationship between job stress and incivility behaviors ($r = .14$, $p < .01$) and revealed that employees with increased levels of workplace stress engaged in acts of incivility. Employees with higher levels of psychological capital exhibited less incivility interactions than employees with lower levels.

The study results also showed that job stress is a problem and contributes to incivility in the workplace. Being overwhelmed with job demands, workloads and deadlines may be a direct cause of stress in the workplace and negative responses to stress.[190,117] Roberts et al.[117] suggested that psychological capital may be a coping strategy to teach employees how to respond positively to job stress and create a positive work environment.

Oore et al.[119] tested whether incivility acts as a moderator of the stressors and strains among hospital workers. Four hundred and seventy-eight health care professionals from 17 care units in Nova Scotia and Ontario were recruited to participate in the study. Participants included 52.9% staff nurses, 7.9% ward clerks, 5.9% physicians, 5.2% licensed practical nurses, 3.6% registered practical nurses and 2% of other health care professionals. The study results reported by Oore et al.[119] were similar to that of Roberts et al.[117] The results revealed that workplace incivility exacerbated work-related stressors and strains in the health care staff. The study conclusions reiterated the importance of minimizing incivility to reduce the impact of work-related stressors.

Stress among health care providers is profound.[120,191] Emergency department staff cope with work-related stressors triggered by the work environment.[120] Healy and Tyrell[120] conducted a literature review on the attitudes and experiences of workplace stress from doctors and nurses in three emergency departments in Ireland. A descriptive survey design was used to gather and study the experiences and attitudes of 103 emergency room nurses and doctors regarding workplace stress. Out of 103 participants, 13% were doctors (62% male, 38% female), 87% were female registered nurses and 9% were male registered nurses.

Healy and Tyrell's[120] findings indicated that work environment played a key role in the development of stress among 51% of the participants. Seventy-five percent of the respondents expressed that the work environment was the factor that made the greatest contribution to their stress. Participants validated the following themes: Poor rostering, workloads, traumatic events and lack of teamwork.

Furthermore, 76% of the participants stated they had no assistance from their employer in dealing with work-related stress. Of that number, 27% stated the assistance was inadequate and 25% believed the assistance offered by the employers was very inadequate. Nearly all the respondents (97%) stated they had experienced work-related stress in the emergency department, which suggested that work-related stress is a problem in countries besides the United States.

The results emphasized that stressful events at work can have profound effects on employees who are often not prepared to cope with work-related stressors. The findings were consistent with those from previous studies that emphasized work-related stressors (job demands), inappropriate work environment (violence), inappropriate behaviors (bullying) and lack of coping strategies.[46,121,119,123]

There is a misconception that nurses work in a safe environment.[124] In the 21st century, extreme job demands on nurses can foster negative cognitive behavioral reactions and increase the rate of physical illnesses.[125,118] A literature review by Roberts and Grubb[118] investigated the impact of job stress on nurses' health and safety and the contribution of working conditions and characteristics to the development of job stress. Roberts and Grubb[118] attested that nurses who experienced job stress complained of health issues, low morale and turnovers.

The review provided strong evidence of an association between job-related stress and a perceived lack of safety, which impacted nurses' health and wellbeing in different nursing settings. Roberts and Grubb[118] suggested that employing a person-focused model may build nurses' abilities to cope with stress, and that an organization-focused model is a critical strategy that may prevent stressful working conditions in nursing. Using a person-focused approach is applicable to specific working conditions in which interpersonal conflict is an issue. An organization-focused model is designed to prevent stressful working conditions and improve workplace morale. Organizational and family support play a role in the ability to manage daily work activities in stressful environments.

NURSING SCHOOL ENVIRONMENT

Incivility is a term that is often used to describe certain bullying behaviors and includes verbal and physical abuse that may occur in the workplace and in learning environments.[109] Bullying behaviors in the form of incivility influence the nursing school learning environment and spreads into nursing practice, affecting both patients and student nurses.[121] Chekwa and Thomas[126] surveyed 50 online students at Troy University to explore students' understanding of the difference between harassment and bullying. The finding was that 47% of the students did not perceive a difference between harassment and bullying. Because of the indistinguishable definitions, respondents have difficulties expressing experiences of bullying and seeking justice.

In a qualitative study Anthony and Yastik[127] explored bullying experiences of nursing students in a clinical setting, perceptions of staff nurses regarding disruptive behaviors and perceptions of the methods that nursing schools used to correct staff nurses' negative behaviors. Participants were selected from a large Midwestern university nursing school. Twenty-one nursing students participated in the focus group study. The results contained three key themes that nursing students used to described experiences with staff nurses: "We" [nursing students] are "in the way," "we" are always in tears and "they" [the staff nurses] just walk away.[127] The consensus among the students was that staff nurses were hostile, dismissive and disinterested, causing the students to feel like outsiders.

Nursing students who are bullied during training may engage in bullying tactics in the nursing practice.[128] In order to understand the problem of bullying in nursing schools, Clarke, Kane, Rajacich and Lafreniere[129] used a descriptive quantitative approach to examine Canadian baccalaureate nursing students' nursing education for origins of bullying acts. Participants consisted of 674 nursing students.

According to the study results 88.7% of students revealed they had encountered a least one act of bullying, 60.2% reported that nursing staff disparaged their efforts to learn the profession and 45.3% expressed they had received negative comments about becoming a nurse. 42.1% stated they had faced hostility while 40.4% reported being unfairly judged. The primary sources of the bullying acts were clinical instructors (30.2%) and staff nurses (25.5%). Clarke et al.[129] suggested that bullying does occur in educational programs and nursing students are at risk of being bullied by nurses and faculty.

Marchiondo, Marchiondo and Lasiter[130] conducted a cross-sectional survey in the United States to examine the effects of uncivil behavior by faculty on student satisfaction with their nursing program. The researchers recruited 152 senior baccalaureate nursing students from two Midwestern universities to participate. Results indicated that 88% of the students experienced at least one instance of uncivil behavior from faculty. Of that 88%, 60% reported that behaviors occurred in a classroom setting, 50% reported experiencing uncivil behaviors in a clinical setting and 43% reported that the mistreatments occurred in different locations (e.g., classroom and clinical settings).

A strong relationship between bullying and dissatisfaction existed among students who experienced uncivil acts by faculty. Regardless of the origin, types or frequencies of bullying experienced, nursing students interpret uncivil acts as rude, insulting and embarrassing.[121] Incidences of bullying behaviors from teachers in nursing schools could possibly result in nursing students contributing to violent acts when they are in the workplace.[73]

Clark and Springer[122] used an exploratory descriptive approach to solicit perceptions of 126 academic nurse leaders from bachelor nursing schools in a Western state about their role in incivility and stressors among faculty and students. The study results revealed that 48.3% of the faculty believed the two highest stressors for students were juggling different roles and demands from work, home and school; 29.7% believed the most important stressor was financial pressure. Faculty reported a 63.4% frequency of student-led uncivil behaviors and in-class disruptions. For instance, 24% of the faculty claimed to have received rude comments, 14% said students were distracted by cell phones and 11.3% had attendance problems such as arriving late and leaving early.

Clark and Springer[122] pointed out that 63.5% of staff reported multiple work demands, while 28.2% who reported heavy workload and inequality as the greatest stressors. In regard to incivility, faculty (80%) were more likely to display negative behaviors toward each other than toward students (20%).

Nursing students frequently encounter horizontal bullying in nursing education.[131] Palaz[132] examined four baccalaureate nursing programs in three different Turkish states using the short version of the Negative Acts Questionnaire (NAQ). Three hundred and seventy nursing students participated in the study and 60% reported encountering at least one bullying behavior during their education as described on the NAQ score. 86.2% were bullied by an older nurse and 92.4% were females perpetrators. Bullying behaviors by faculty members are destructive to the nursing profession because faculty bullying denies students positive role models and the chance to develop compassion and empathy for others.

Nursing leaders from academic and clinic settings must partner to understand more completely the complex bullying effects on the professional culture, the intricacies of the teaching-learning environment, practices to overcome the perception of uncaring and the preparation of novice nurses.[132,24] The findings by Palaz[132] added to the literature regarding the importance of raising awareness about coping methods and the perception of how students in nursing education may affect existing nursing practices.

ॐ

HORIZONTAL AND LATERAL VIOLENCE

Bullying acts in the nursing profession include lateral and horizontal violence. Wilson, Diedrich, Phelps and Choi[133] explained that horizontal and lateral violence is a form of nurse-nurse hostility in the nursing profession (e.g. disrespectful communications, sabotage, withholding of information, passive-aggressive behavior). Definitions of lateral and horizontal violence have, over time, formed a continuum of interchangeable definitions including overt and covert actions, physical violence and interpersonal conflict that consists of nonphysical abuse.[188, 189] Lateral and horizontal violence display similar behaviors and may be described as interchangeable. One subtle difference is that lateral targets their peers (peer-to-peer) whereas horizontal violence is a power position (supervisor-to-subordinate). The incidence and prevalence of horizontal violence in the nursing profession are undetermined because horizontal violence is not consistently reported by nurses.[131, 178, 179]

In a descriptive, quasi-experimental study conducted by Stagg, Sheridan, Jones and Speroni,[171] 62 medical and surgical nurses completed an Internet-based survey to determine the following: The frequency of bullying among medical and surgical nurses and increased knowledge about the bullying behaviors achieved by using the response to cognitive rehearsal training program. The participants were recruited from two rural community hospitals. Among the participants, 80% experienced bullying, 75% reported bullying incidents occurred while working in the medical units and 57% stated the bullying acts were from their colleagues. Of the 62 medical and surgical nurses, 24% participated in a cognitive rehearsal program that consisted of a 2-hour session with pre and post-tests. According to Stagg et al.,[171] 80% of the nurses reported that the concept of workplace bullying was broad and the rehearsal program expanded their comprehension of bullying.

In a cross-sectional model testing study, Purpora, Blegen and Stotts[172] explored the relationship between hospital staff nurses' beliefs about themselves and their reflections of horizontal violence. One hundred and seventy-five actively licensed registered nurses were recruited from a list obtained from the California Board of Registered Nursing (CABRN) to participate in an online survey.

Twenty-one registered nurses stated they had experienced horizontal violence daily or weekly during the previous six months. 12.6% reported they had been asked to perform duties below their level of competence, been subject to unreasonable deadlines (1.4%), had opinions ignored (9.9%) or were generally ignored (9.2%). The nurses revealed they had experienced subtle negative acts. One-seventh of the nurses experienced finger-pointing, violation of personal space, practical jokes and allegations. The study results revealed that nurses who hold negative thoughts about themselves, work situations and oppression are at risk of experiencing horizontal violence.

In a mixed method descriptive study, Walrafen et al.[189] solicited the experiences of 227 nurses in a multi-institutional health care system to understand the complexities of horizontal violence. Participants completed a nine-item horizontal violence behavior survey and answered three additional open-ended questions. The findings of the quantitative survey indicated that 77% of nurses witnessed backstabbing, 72% experienced nonverbal negative innuendo and bickering between nurses and 76% endured other privacy violations.

Among the participants, 58% of the nurses personally experienced nonverbal negative innuendos and backstabbing.

Walrafen et al.[189] identified three themes into which horizontal violence can be categorized: Sadly caught up in the moment, overt and covert maltreatment and commitment to positive change in their workplace. Based on the results reported by Walrafen et al.,[189] continuous dialogue and intervention is needed to address horizontal violence in patient care delivery organizations.

In an effort to understand the prevalence of horizontal violence in the hospital environment and the effects on nurse attrition, Wilson et al.[133] investigated hostility also known as lateral violence and bullying. The purpose of the retrospective descriptive study was twofold: To explore the degree of incidents of horizontal hostility and ascertain new nurses' intentions to resign.

One-hundred-thirty nurses participated from inpatient units. Of the surveyed participants, 90.7% were women, of whom 50% had worked in the health care workforce for approximately 10 years. 83.1% (n = 108) of nurses had witnessed bullying behaviors among nurses in the unit and 61% (n = 53) reported being bullied by physicians. Wilson et al.[133] found that 90% (n = 110) of the nurses reported difficulty in confronting bullying individuals, whereas 10% reported having no problem confronting the aggressor. When asked what influenced the increase in sick time, 95% of the nurses believed that horizontal hostility influenced absenteeism, increased turnovers rates and reduced job satisfaction; 39.6% cited horizontal hostility as the reason for voluntary resignation of employment.

COPING STRATEGIES FOR WORKPLACE BULLYING AND STRESS

Exposure to stress within nursing practice and education has been reported in several studies.[135,119] Bullying, incivility and negative working conditions have been well established as sources that foster an extraordinarily stressful environment for nurses in both health care and nursing education.[2] Considering the volume of complaints from nurses regarding consequences of workplace stress, coping strategies to mitigate bullying behaviors must be a priority for the nursing profession.

Civility is one recommendation to reduce workplace stress among health care workers.[119] Oore et al.[119] believed that introducing civility as an intervention may assist in coping with the inherent stress related to work. Person-focused and organization-focused stress reduction is another effective intervention to implement once sources have been identified.[118] Integrating both approaches may be effective in diminishing job-related stressors for nurses and other similar professions. Roberts and Grubbs[118] described a person-focused approach as an intervention that promotes stronger and positive individual outcomes, whereas an organization-focused plan promotes positive organizational outcomes.

Workplace stress is a major barrier within nursing practice. Health care organizations are "social systems.[136]" Working collaboratively is essential for organizations to function and create a healthy working culture.[137] Nursing managers at all levels have a duty and responsibility to identify strategies to reduce bullying acts, promote awareness of bullying and provide ongoing healthy work environment training.[137] A lack of bullying-prevention training programs exists in the nursing profession to reduce work-related stress, provide emotional and organizational support and promote job satisfaction.[111,138,139,140]

Dealing with workplace bullying and stress requires that management provide resources to address the problem holistically (e.g., personal experiences, emotions and personal lives).[141] The purpose of the study by Wright[141] was to examine the role of communication competence in terms of predicting conflict style, job satisfaction, job stress and job burnout among 221 health care workers. The results indicated that higher communication competence scores, using Wiemann's 36-item communication competence scale, were predictive of integrating and obliging conflict styles among health care workers, while lower communication competence scores were predictive of dominating and avoiding conflict styles. In addition, an integrating conflict style was predictive of reduced stress and increased job satisfaction whereas dominating and avoiding conflict styles were predictive of increased job burnout among the participants.

Effective resources must be made available for nurses to learn how to identify and develop individualized and effective coping strategies in order to reduce occurrences of bullying.[107,118,141] Although organizations often take responsibility for bullying in the nursing practice, Wright[141] believed that nurses must take an active role in their personal health and evaluate whether nursing is a good fit.

In 2012, Ashker et al.[135] explored coping strategies for work-related stressors used by nurses working in dialysis units. The study had a dual purpose: To identify and describe 19 hemodialysis nurses' emotional stressors and the coping strategies for emotional wellbeing used in the daily work environment. To measure coping strategies, a descriptive design and a "ways of coping" questionnaire were used. The 19 participants were recruited from six hemodialysis centers in Midwestern United States. Ashker et al.[135] stated that the results of the study were influenced by the inexperience of the nurses and their answers to coping questions.

Ashker et al.'s[135] findings identified eight coping strategies for self-control and other options to handle work-related occurrences used by nurses:

- Planful (i.e., having many plans) problem solving,
- self-controlling,
- positive reappraisal,

- social support structures,
- responsibility acceptance,
- confrontative coping,
- distancing and
- escape-avoidance.

The results indicated that 25% of nurses working in the hemodialysis units used planful problem solving and self-controlling as coping techniques when encountering job-related stressors. Although planful problem solving and self-controlling ranked the highest, Ashker et al.[135] suggested that more than one coping strategy may be applied to workplace stressors.

A qualitative exploratory study conducted by Happell et al.[193] examined how nurses cope with workplace stress outside the work environment. The aim of the study was to identify coping techniques used by nurses away from the workplace. Thirty-eight registered nurses from various units within an acute care hospital were recruited to participate. The results revealed 11 types of dysfunctional and functional coping strategies for work-related stressors, categorized into four coping themes: Substance abuse, socializing with colleagues, engaging in other activities and antisocial behaviors. Substance abuse was a commonly reported coping strategy among the nurse focus group, especially the use of alcohol and cigarettes as substances of choice.

The group of nurses described socializing with co-workers as another coping strategy, including social clubs and social networks and engaging in outdoor and physical activities to relieve the stress from work. Antisocial behaviors consisted of avoiding others and displacement. Substance abuse coping strategies presented in the study have potential health consequences. Social events were occasionally identified as ineffective, and participants often opted for avoidance and isolation. Personal and interpersonal factors, organizational structure and professional stressors were all variables that played an enormous role in the cause of job-related stress among nurses.

Reducing the effects of bullying behaviors requires effective training.[142,42,143] Building a learning culture and team collegiality is a technique that needs a clear direction in the nursing profession. Effective training on coping strategies identifies best practices to the change process with staff. Without effective training strategies, nurses may develop coping skills that do not prepare them for future occurrences of bullying among nurses.[42] A systemic review conducted by Stagg and Sheridan[42] about different disciplines such as business, education and health care compared the effectiveness of intervention to manage bullying in the workplace.

Four workplace training strategies were identified to prevent or manage bullying in the health care workplace: Mentoring programs, cognitive rehearsal, assertiveness versus aggression, piloted aggression and violence minimization modules. Implementation of the previous strategies was found to be effective, as it stopped bullying behaviors, improved nurses' coping skills, increased participants' confidence in addressing bullying incidents and improved colleague relationships through effective communication, collaboration and conflict resolution. These findings confirm that confronting and overcoming bullying behaviors have a positive effect on reducing the impact of workplace bullying.

WORKPLACE TRAINING NEEDS

Workplace bullying may be reduced or prevented when employees receive training on self-protection strategies.[125] Learning coping strategies and conflict-resolution skills may strengthen nurses' interpersonal relationships, promote positive patient outcomes, reduce burnout, reduce emotional stress and influence a patient-safety culture in nursing practice.[144]

Training and other interventions addressing the aftermath responses may improve safety of patients.[125] In the literature review conducted by Livington et al.,[125] the common training practices discussed in the primary research were verbal and nonverbal de-escalation strategies, control, restraint or seclusion skills, prediction/prevention of aggression and limited search on staff training that included reporting occurrences. Livington et al.[125] believed that results from training programs were not effective because of the poorly designed curriculum, lack of standardization and improper fit to the specific work setting. In contrast to Stagg & Sheridan's[42] findings, an effective training program for nursing staff increases nurses' knowledge about how to manage aggression or bullying behaviors in the workplace.

Workplace Violence Awareness and Prevention for Employers and Employees[145] recommended that de-escalation training be used to deal with bullying interactions. An annual review of training needs by human resources personnel should be conducted to ensure that bullying reduction practices continue and to provide a prevention strategies refresher course about prior training sessions. An additional level of bullying prevention needs to be the primary focus to reduce negative effects on health care providers' personal lives, patient safety and workplace environments.[146]

Strandmark and Rahm[139] conducted a focus group interview with 36 health care professionals that consisted of 13 nursing aides, 3 mental health care aides, 1 pediatric nursing aid, 2 care assistants, 6 nurses and 1 social worker. The participants in Strandmark and Rahm's[139] study worked in eldercare wards at two nursing homes and on a geriatric psychiatric ward at a hospital. The researchers aimed to develop and implement an intervention program as a way to combat bullying in the workplace. The intervention and implementation of a humanistic value system consisted of four focus groups. All participants were placed into small groups for lecture and training about the definition and consequences of bullying. While they did not specifically address coping skills, all participants concurred that a zero-tolerance policy was needed, along with a focus on a learning organization as a means of mitigating bullying.

Strandmark and Rahm[139] reported that the training was an effective vehicle to increase awareness of the risks for bullying whereas, in the beginning, the hospital and nursing homes had no existing policy on bullying conflicts which contributed to bullying. All participants believed that lectures and small group training appeared to be the most effective means of combating bullying. The recommendation offered by Strandmark and Rahm[139] for a successful health care organization is to integrate a training program that includes problem solving to reduce bullying.

Workplace bullying prevention and intervention training programs are scarce in the health care industry literature.[138] Providing training to health care professionals on appropriate ways to respond to bullying is imperative, especially for individuals who frequently report bullying acts.[123] Bullies may model bullying behavior tactics from past nursing instructors, work aggression or other learned behaviors. Health care professionals are not equipped to adequately address inappropriate behaviors proactively without resorting to retaliation.[123] According to Simon and Sauer,[123] individuals who experience higher incidents of bullying are unlikely to have had effective training or resources to confront bullying acts.

In 2004, the U.S. Department of Labor Occupational Safety and Health Administration (OSHA)[147] published a general overview of safety training for health care workers, which includes violence prevention training. According to OSHA,[147] "Every employee should understand the concept of 'universal precautions for violence' to be avoided or mitigated through preparation." A combination of formal training for individuals on personal safety and professional assault-response can prevent bullying incident in the workplace. The health care environment is complex and not well suited for traditional status quo training programs. Quinlan et al.[138] stated that for health care organizations to be fully operative and successful, a leader needs to be proactive in developing staff training programs to reduce bullying in the workplace. The results of Quinlan et al.'s[138] study indicated a need for research into staff training instruments to reduce the long-term effects of bullying.

UNSAFE PATIENT ENVIRONMENT

In nursing, acknowledgement of health care staff behavior is important when examining threats to patient safety.[148,49,149] Wyatt[150] stated that "Individuals who have a history of disruptive behavior also pose the highest litigation risk for American hospitals." Bullying in the workplace has been associated with increased mediation errors, work-related injuries and low rates of reporting medication errors.[49]

Staff disruptive behaviors (e.g., bullying, incivilty, horizontal and lateral violence) compromise the delivery of patient care and are directly related to poor clinical outcome.[149] Longo and Hain[149] provided a overview of bullying and approaches of reducing bullying acts in health care systems. In a single participant case study, "Liz's Story," which exemplified a hemodialysis clinical setting, Longo and Hain[149] identified participant behaviors reported by other health care workers. One technician reported that "I try not to schedule myself when I know she will be in charge" and "several staff quit," which led to a staff shortage and reflected the poor quality of care. As Longo and Hain[149] concluded, a healthy work environment is a fundamental component of addressing bullying acts within a nursing setting and eventually results in a safe patient care environment.

In 2008, the Joint Commission Accreditation of Healthcare Organizations[151] (JCAHO) published an alert that addressed behaviors that impaired an otherwise healthy work environment and created a safety risk for patients and staff. In the alert, the JCAHO[151] report noted that when such inappropriate behaviors occur, certain areas comprise a potential threat to patient safety including medical errors (e.g., medication), poor patient care, increased costs of care delivery and nurse attrition. McNamara[152] conducted a review of two studies that focused on hospital nurses' disruptive and bullying behaviors and the impact on patient outcomes. The literature review results indicated that disruptive or bullying acts fostered 67% of adverse events and medical errors, 58% compromised patient safety, 68% led to poor quality of care and 28% resulted in patient mortality.

Laschinger[49] investigated the impact of bullying and workplace mistreatment among Canadian nurses and their perceptions of patient safety risk, quality of care and prevalence of adverse events. Three-hundred-thirty-six acute care nurses completed quantitative questionnaires early in 2013. Descriptive statistics were used to measure nurses' exposure to bullying. A score of 0.59 (SD 1.45) indicated that nurses were not exposed to bullying and a score of 1.04 (SD 2.31) indicated that patients are less likely to be at risk for unsafe patient care due to bullying acts. The results indicated that direct and indirect bullying behaviors had unfavorable effects on the quality of care. In the same study, the researchers revealed that physicians' bullying acts affected patient adverse events, patients' safety risk and quality of care. Laschinger[49] believed that negative interaction (e.g., lack of communication) among physicians, nurses and other team members hindered the potential for providing high quality care.

CONCLUSIONS BASED ON THE LITERATURE REVIEW

The findings from the literature review confirm a strong relationship exists between bullying, stress, the development of psychological conditions (e.g., PTSD) and patient safety issues. Nurses report more work-related accidents, stress and a lack of coping strategies to control bullying behaviors and relieve the psychological distress compared to other health care workers.[106] Bullying victims have also reported symptoms of depression and suicidal ideation.[105]

The literature reviewed illustrated the prevalence of horizontal violence and bullying and validated that a direct relationship exists between bullying behaviors at work and in learning environments (e.g., nursing programs). High-stress work environments and repeated exposure to bullying events may affect productivity, have unfavorable effects on health care professionals' physical and psychological wellbeing, may reduce nurses' quality of life and satisfaction with the work environment and may place patient safety at risk.[149] The literature reviewed also indicated that nurses must have effective coping strategies to manage work-related bullying.

CHAPTER TWO SUMMARY

Employees in health care organizations may experience bullying and work-related stress during their tenure with the employer. Face-to-face confrontations, workplace stress and lateral or horizontal bullying results in victims who feel ashamed, humiliated or threatened and who may engage in desperate behaviors if they do not perceive a workplace culture that values caring, relationships or empathy.[153,81] The effects of bullying and stress appear to be linked to unstable emotions and psychological health disturbances.[57]

Bullying behaviors and job-related stressors are associated with psychological and physical health disturbances in individuals. The findings from multiple studies[154] consistently indicated that individuals who have experienced bullying exhibit more mental health disturbances than non-victims; individuals who have experienced bullying at an early age have the highest level of suicide attempts. Scholars have predicted that individuals will develop psychiatric problems and comorbidities because of exposure to bullying.[79,15]

Documentation is lacking for approaches used to address the growing problem of bullying in health care organizations. Current training programs have shown inconsistent methods to address workplace aggression and prevention of workplace bullying that were not designed to reflect nurses' needs in a hospital setting. Early detection is important in addressing bullying and avoiding adverse mental health outcomes. The literature review presented here reveals a gap in extant knowledge about the best ways to combat workplace bullying. In particular, it highlights the need to have a clear, effective and consistent method for the development or implementation of bullying prevention strategies. These issues were addressed as a part of the present study.

Chapter Two Notes

CHAPTER THREE

METHOD

$\mathcal{I}$n an effort to explore bullying dynamics in health care, qualitative design may yield further understanding of the bullying behaviors that occur in acute care settings and specific impacts on patients and nurses. A qualitative methodology focuses on moving beyond existing knowledge to interpret social circumstance, perception of experiences and learning about participants' histories of everyday world experiences.[32] Registered nurses who have experienced or witnessed bullying on the job were recruited to participate in interviews to foster an understanding of the stressors related to bullying in the workplace. The participants were three RNs in the pilot study and 14 RNs in the main study who were from the greater Oklahoma City area. All participants were employed in acute care hospital settings.

In this qualitative study, a purposive sampling strategy was used to sample nurses who could provide firsthand experiences and perceptions about bullying. The data gathered during participant telephone interviews may be used to develop new strategies for nursing leaders to encourage a positive work environment, increase job satisfaction and decrease the psychological impacts of bullying among nurses. Information received from study participants may address the gap in knowledge regarding job-related stress and the perceived effects of bullying on the personal and professional lives of nurses in acute care settings.

RESEARCH METHOD APPROPRIATENESS

The qualitative method supports the study of behaviors and actions of human beings in a natural setting.[155] A qualitative method provides multiple ways to interpret participants' experiences including feelings, thoughts and beliefs from their world.[156,157] Unlike quantitative methods and approaches, a qualitative method facilitates holistic analysis and understanding of the world as perceived by participants, who help define and explain phenomena as they have experienced them.[159,158] Exploratory qualitative research is appropriate when limited prior research exists about a topic. For the purpose of the study, the qualitative method was used to elicit relevant information and insights from the nurse participants.

Qualitative research findings may help health care leaders improve their understanding of employees' thoughts and perceptions. Nurses who work in inpatient acute care settings had an opportunity to share their experiences and their perspectives of work-related bullying that precipitates negative impacts on personal and professional wellbeing and patient safety.

The qualitative approach allowed participating nurses to communicate personal perception and experiences of bullying in the workplace. Firsthand descriptions of bullying led to identification of themes and expanded the understanding of bullying in the workplace. Qualitative methods permit investigators to gather data about participants' emotions, thoughts, experiences and meanings connected to the studied phenomenon.[159] Salkind[160] asserted that the intent of qualitative research is to examine participants' behaviors and to analyze themes emerging from questions to gain an in-depth understanding of the phenomenon being studied.

Historically, quantitative research has been the method of choice for studies of nursing.[161] Researchers use quantitative research to quantify patient care, measure statistical variables and test hypotheses in nursing.[161] Berg,[38] Leech and Onwuegbuzie[162] and Leedy and Ormrod[37] espoused that quantitative methods may result in providing a superficial understanding of participants' experiences and thoughts and would require a large sample size. Quantitative methods focus on causal relationships, values and frequencies of phenomena suitable for clinical trials, cohort studies and closed-ended questionnaire surveys.[163] Because the aim of this dissertation study was not to explore how many nurses experienced the studied phenomenon or to determine causality, but rather to describe and interpret the shared experiences of bullying from the participants' perspectives, a quantitative method was not suitable. The data collected focused on participants' viewpoints on bullying behaviors, job-related stressors and training experiences in hospital organizations.

RESEARCH DESIGN APPROPRIATENESS

Exploratory research depends on a detailed literature review and rich textural data to gain insight into participants' experiences.[164] Exploratory research is appropriate to examine an existing problem to gain a deeper understanding of participants' experiences and perceptions regarding the studied phenomenon.[53,157] In an effort to explore new knowledge, Hammer[165] stated that the exploratory inquiry design allows for obtaining information that focuses on increasing knowledge and revealing new ideas that have potential for future research.

The goal of this exploratory inquiry was to explore inpatient nurses' perceptions of work-related stressors that precipitate bullying acts, the impact on patient safety and to identify what training is needed for nurses to decrease workplace bullying. Developing new guidelines is not warranted during analysis of the data gleaned from the exploratory design but may be appropriate for further investigation.

According to Berg,[38] the focus of exploratory research is to extract the essence of an experience. Exploratory research is an avenue for the collection of detailed descriptions of a phenomenon that all study participants have experienced. An exploratory inquiry is dependent on the existence of the problem and a researcher's perception of the existing gap in knowledge. The approach chosen for this study was used to explore first-person descriptive narrative of participants' experiences with bullying acts as described by Ivey.[166] According to Husserl,[167] a qualitative approach leads to a logical, coherent design that provides details of perceived perceptions of a phenomenon. In this dissertation study, the results offered nurses' perspectives of a shared or common experience of bullying that may help them identify and cope with future bullying in the clinical setting.

POPULATION

According the Oklahoma Board of Nursing (OBN)[168] annual report, 51,266 registered nurses were licensed in Oklahoma. The general population consists of 33,924 licensed nurses employed in

Oklahoma; the specific population from which a sample was selected totaled 5,497 RNs working in Oklahoma City metropolitan hospitals. The sample was purposively selected to allow the phenomenon to be explored in different nursing departments within the inclusion criteria.

One avenue for gaining potential participants was through the Oklahoma Board of Nursing, as described in the sampling frame. Nurses were asked three questions related to the inclusion criteria and, based on the responses, nurses who meet the requirements were provided an initial recruitment letter about the purpose and nature of the study. In addition, study participants were selected based on purposive sampling criteria appropriate for recruiting the required number of participants. In order to meet the study inclusion criteria, the nurses had to respond affirmatively to the following questions:

- Are you actively employed in an acute care nursing unit?
- Have you experienced workplace training regarding bullying?
- Would you like to take part in the study?

GEOGRAPHIC AREA

The study participants were RNs working in inpatient acute care hospital settings (e.g., surgical, oncology, etc.) in the metropolitan area of Oklahoma City, which consists of the following seven counties: Canadian, Cleveland, Grady, Lincoln, Logan, McClain and Oklahoma. According to the United States Census Bureau[169] as of July 1, 2013, an estimate of the Oklahoma City population was 610,613. The reported population by race in 2013 was as follows: White, 62.7%; African American, 15.1%; Hispanic, 17.2%;

American Indian, 3.5%; Asian, 4.0%; Native Hawaiian and other Pacific Islander, 0.1%; and two or more races, 5.2%.

CHAPTER THREE SUMMARY

The qualitative inquiry method was appropriate to examine individuals' experiences captured in semi-structured interviews and to explore the meaning of the experiences. Chapter Three includes an explanation of the research method, the design appropriateness, the study population and sample. The study, based on methods associated with explorative inquiry, was conducted with 14 RNs from acute care nursing settings in the greater Oklahoma City area. The sample was generated using a purposive method. Application of thematic analysis steps supported the process of data analysis. The data consisted of recorded interviews and field notes. Credibility, transferability, validity and confirmability provided process rigor and validation of the findings.

Chapter Three Notes

CHAPTER FOUR

RESULTS

*T*he purpose of this qualitative exploratory study was to explore workplace training that nurses received regarding bullying, nurses' perceptions regarding the effectiveness of that training, their ability to cope with bullying and suggested areas for improved training regarding bullying. In addition, nurses' perceptions regarding how bullying impacts patient safety and their ability to do their jobs was explored. Chapter Four includes a dialogue of the results of this exploratory qualitative inquiry dissertation study. Detailed information was gathered from 14 licensed registered nurses who worked in hospitals in the Oklahoma City metropolitan area. Research participants consisted of 12 females and 2 males.

PILOT STUDY

Data for this pilot study were obtained from the first two females who met the inclusion criteria for the main study. The two selected registered nurses answered the interview questions and provided feedback about the interview questions and interview process. After each interview, the participants were asked to offer suggestions how to improve the interview questions and process in order to elicit sufficient data to address the purpose of the study.

The following interview questions were asked during the pilot interview:

1. Tell me about the training on workplace bullying at your current place of employment.
2. What have been some of the benefits of the training? Can you give some examples?
3. What have been some of the shortcomings of the training? Can you give some examples?
4. How has the training on bullying influenced your job performance in your specialty area? Can you give some examples? What is your specialty area?
5. How has workplace training on bullying helped you cope with bullying? Follow up question: What coping strategies have you used?
6. In your opinion, how has training on workplace bullying impacted bullying acts at your hospital?
7. How has the workplace training on bullying influenced your ability to maintain standards regarding patient safety? Can you give some examples?
8. What do you think would improve workplace training for nurses to help reduce future bullying?
9. What other comments would you would like to share regarding bullying and workplace training?

The interview protocol followed in the pilot study was identical to that adopted in the main research study. Pilot study participants commented that the interview questions were adequate and sufficiently thorough for the main study. Analysis of the pilot study participant responses revealed that no changes were necessary.

DEMOGRAPHICS OF PARTICIPANTS

The items included in the demographic section of the survey sought to elicit participants' titles, gender, years of nursing experience and area of specialty. In terms of gender distribution, the study sample was comprised of 12 females and 2 males. In addition, 79% of the participating nurses indicated they had 10 or less years of experience, while the remaining 21% had 15 or more years of nursing experience. When asked to state their current position, 6 of the 14 respondents indicated that they worked in medical surgical units, three worked in ICUs and two were employed in ERs. The three remaining respondents had positions in psychology, OB and neurology units.

DATA COLLECTION AND ANALYSIS

Research Question 1

RQ1 asked "How have workplace training programs influenced the ability, or inability, of RNs to respond to bullying in inpatient hospital settings?" To investigate RQ1, the interviewees were asked several questions that allowed them to discuss this issue in depth. Participants were prompted using the following guiding statements and questions:

- Tell me about the training on workplace bullying at your current place of employment. What have been some of the benefits of the training?
- What have been some of the shortcomings of the training?
- In your opinion, how has training on workplace bullying impacted bullying acts at your hospital?

When answering interview questions, research participants were reminded that they should reflect on their personal experiences with workplace bullying and the impact of training they received on the way they dealt with these incidents. All 14 participants voiced concern with the lack of standardization in the training aimed at eradicating bullying from their units. Thirteen participants also indicated the lack of standardization contributes to the pervasiveness of unacceptable behavior in the workplace because victims have no official reporting channels, whereas perpetrators have no immediate consequences. Thirteen of the participants appraised the training received as a hindrance to the adoption of nursing practice norms and attitudes.

Due to the inconsistency in the definitions of bullying and lack of pertinent information, the nurses felt unprepared to address bullying behaviors and mitigate their effects on nursing practice. The participants' sense of helplessness undermined their self-confidence and their preparedness to support others, potentially undermining patient safety.

All participants had received some workplace anti-bullying training in various forms, including online continuing education. Hospitals also provided computerized learning modules, in-services, flyers or posters and videos. Thirteen participants were unsure if they had actually received training specifically targeting bullying.

Because of the inconsistencies in the language used in the training program to discuss bullying, it was difficult to establish commonalities in the participants' narratives pertaining to the anti-bullying training they received. Examples of ambiguous language concerned with training included terminology such as "a Code of Conduct" and "professional development." Thirteen of the 14 participants indicated the workplace anti-bullying training they received was minimal and typically focused on patients instead of employees. In addition, all 14 participants questioned the effectiveness of the delivery format which they regarded as a single, and rather lengthy, annual education session inappropriate for imparting the practical tools for combating bullying in the workplace. Thirteen participants stated that annual training initiatives were not an effective preventive measure for reaching an optimal outcome for their organization or their specific department.

Table 1 summarizes the participants' perceptions of the effectiveness of the workplace anti-bullying training offered within their respective health care organization.

Table 1

Ineffectiveness of Workplace Anti-bullying Training (N = 14)

Major themes related to bullying training received	N	%
Challenges of uniformity	14	100
Lack of resources	13	93
Limitation of the education	13	93
Lack of consistent definition of bullying	13	93

In support of the findings reported in Table 1, some

characteristic responses offered by the participants during their interviews are noted.

Participant RN01 described workplace anti-bullying training as follows:

> A continuing education credit. You go through, it makes you aware of it, it defines it, and then it doesn't really give people the tools that they need to be able to deal with it when it's happening. I think it just makes you aware of it, but I don't think that it really. I think it's only brought awareness, but not prevention.

When asked to define or describe perception of workplace bullying and effects of the training, participant RN14 shared the following:

> There's a section on sexual harassment or any kind of harassment that bleeds over a little bit. You answer 10 questions on a pre-test. If you don't get 100% then it will throw up another test of five questions and you can take that test endlessly until you get 100%. The questions are very simplistic. It's very annoying. I don't think it makes any difference whatsoever in how people actually interact with one another.

Although RN14's observation was related to online training, similar views were shared by participants who attended classroom-based sessions. For example, participant RN08 described the training received as follows:

> Just like an in-service type situation, where they go over. They define bullying, and what it looks like, and how to report it. You meet in a classroom and then they go over the PowerPoint. They talk about what it looks like, because most people think it's like outright just being mean, but sometimes it can be like scheduling one person to maybe have ten patients

as opposed to another nurse having two, maybe the charge nurse that's favoring. Once you received the training, it definitely helps with handling that type of behavior if it happens.

Participant RN03 offered rather negative views of anti-bullying training received:

We take those classes, yeah. They're our learning module systems that we do annually on the computer system, that are due every year. It's just a repeat of the same thing. I guess for the workplace bullying, they should make it more important. Well one thing is, it's the same one every year. So, you kind of memorize it, so it's meaningless.

Participant RN12 described the workplace anti-bullying training as follows:

It was just a quick video going over basic harassment and sexual harassment. Then like a five to eight question multiple choice. Several short little tests. I believe it's annually. I would say there's no benefits to the training other than it checks a box off, and I can continue on and it doesn't require a lot of effort on our part. I guess it gave me the knowledge. I don't think there needs to be more because I don't feel that the training we get is any good, so why throw more bad training at the situation.

Participant RN11 described training by stating the following:

All the nurses do on a routine basis, and we do cover things under the topics of bullying. It's like a computerized tutorial, and it just goes through: What is bullying? That type of thing, or we often do a bedside huddle or something. It's not really a training tool or anything like that. We just kind of whiz through it, just to check them off. It's not very effective training, to tell you the truth. I feel like they don't do enough of it.

Participant RN10 described the currently available workplace anti-bullying training with the following response:

We just watch a video and answer a few questions at the end of the video. I think basically it was more patient-centered than employee-centered. It [video] gave you some examples of how you can identify if someone is trying to make you do something that you don't feel comfortable doing. I guess, the shortcoming would be even though the information is presented, you know where to go people still aren't feeling comfortable enough. Maybe they don't feel like it's going to be handled effectively or appropriately, the situation. It just helped to identify when someone is trying to force you into doing something that you don't feel comfortable doing or if someone has threatened you in a way.

Participants' experiences of workplace anti-bullying training were not particularly favorable and resulted in diverse viewpoints of what constitutes workplace bullying, as well as the type of training that could effectively eradicate it. In particular, all 14 participants concurred that the anti-bullying training they had attended thus far was overly superficial and not beneficial to their nursing practice. The workplace anti-bullying training that the interviewees had received was delivered through a computerized testing system that did not offer the socialization skills required to address bullying in their workplace.

Analysis of the participants' narratives revealed four major themes that were discussed by the interviewees. The themes were:

- Challenges stemming from lack of uniformity in the definition of bullying (n = 14)
- Lack of resources (n = 13)

- Lack of examples of language that could constitute bullying (n =13) and
- Limitations of the anti-bullying education (n = 13).

All interviewees indicated that although workplace anti-bullying training was offered, the training did not include any guidance on practical resolutions or steps to be taken when faced with bullying incidents. In addition, the curriculum did not specify what constitutes bullying or offensive language. All 14 participants expressed frustration with the method of delivery and the lack of consistent communication within their organizations. All participants agreed that employers should provide effective workplace training on bullying that focuses on bullying prevention and specific guidance for incident reporting and resolution.

❧

Research Question 2

In order to assist the study participants in sharing their views in relation to RQ2, "What is the perceived influence on job performance in inpatient hospital settings of workplace training on bullying?" as a part of their interviews, the nurses responded to the following prompts:

- How has the training on bullying influenced your job performance in your specialty area?
- How has workplace training on bullying helped you cope with bullying?

When the responses yielded by the interviews were subsequently examined, the data indicated the workplace anti-bullying training the participating nurses received in their respective organizations had a limited direct effect on their performance and coping strategies. Thirteen participants felt they had to resort to their moral beliefs and communication skills as a means of coping with bullying behaviors, thus attempting to limit the bullying's effect on their performance and patient safety. Coping strategies that were used by the nurses are summarized in Table 2 and are supported by excerpts from individual interviews for illustration.

Table 2

Coping Strategies Employed by Nurses

Major themes related to coping strategies employed by nurses	N	%
Moral and ethical merits	13	93
Intercommunication	14	100

Research participants spoke of employing civilities as coping techniques, because they felt that this would prepare them for future occurrences of bullying. Civility behaviors expressed by the participants included respect, tolerance, morals, consideration and a common sense approach to conflict.

RN14 stated:

You just know better. I personally don't want to have anything to do with bullying and won't tolerate it in any way on my watch any more than I will tolerate race discrimination because of who I am at a heart/soul level, not because of my training. I function based on a moral compass, not an educational level.

RN08 was of the view that the organization must play a more proactive role in the fight against bullying by holding nurses accountable to the rules. In the words of RN08:

Well, the best thing you can do is to just remain calm and to not take it personal[ly], because the thing about bullying is that it's about the other person, it has nothing to do with you. If that person is not willing to be receptive of what you're trying to tell them, again, you just follow your chain of command.

Participant RN08 further shared the following:

The thing is that, once everybody understands that there's accountability for the type of behavior. Because out of that training there will be a cost if you want to come to work and bully people. You won't work there anymore, so people know there's a consequence. If sometimes when you give a consequence, it kind of curtails their behavior a little bit. I'm just saying there are rules. We just set the limit. We just set the standard.

RN04 agreed that consequences are important, noting that you cannot make everybody happy. RN04 stated:

Everybody is not going to behave the way we think that they should behave. If you do debrief; debriefing's probably about the best thing. Once we share that and we allow them to share their stories.

Participant RN01 specifically commented on the value of the training course attended.

Because of the training module, it made me more aware of it and that: You know, where I work, the motto is, love, learn, and lead. That is the motto. That is what we're taught to do. The love part doesn't come from everybody, but I can learn and I can lead other people. I mean, I can do all three, but that module did help me to be able to lead others. I think the nurses are kind of left to themselves to find coping strategies. I just try to slow my breathing down; I try to listen. When I respond, I talk a lot slower. It helps me to be more calm. Then it kind of slows down, or I say nothing, and/or try to get away from the situation.

Participant RN03 also referred to self-reliance when dealing with bullying at the workplace and related:

I think I went in with a different attitude this time, because of my experience from my last job. I did not use the techniques that were taught me because I was fearful of consequences, so I transferred jobs.

RN03 went on to say:

I think I speak up a little bit more now. Not that I've always been a quiet person, but I think I've learned to tell the person immediately, "Hey, that really upset me." I don't know if that stops the bullying, because it's not a bullying behavior, but it's something that upset me, so I don't allow them to do that to me again.

As coping strategies were further explored within individual interviews, 13 of the research participants echoed drawing upon similar morals and ethical techniques to address bullying behaviors at work.

RN09 suggested the following:

Going back to the whole respect factor and put yourself in somebody else's place. How would you want to be treated? Yes, there are rules that have to be obeyed, but there's ways to go about it. I think a lot of it is being able to talk with your co-workers, developing that bond where you can let it all out, deescalate yourself.

Participant RN11 also held the view that an individual is primarily guided by an inner moral compass when interacting with colleagues. RN11 recalled giving "like a personal in-service to my own unit about bullying. I wanted to at least try to take that information back to my peers. I also became a personal mentor to one of our newer nurses." RN11 described an incident that served as a catalyst for sharing the gathered information with co-workers:

I was witnessing her being bullied and pushed around by some of our nurses. I developed a really great relationship with her, and I tried to encourage her and help her develop some confidence and give her some ideas of how to overcome bullying situations or how she could, not fight back, but deal with the situations.

When asked to comment on the behaviors, RN11 responded, as follows:

I don't get overly upset about it being a bullying situation. Those are other people's actions. On the way home, I can express my emotion then. I've learned to have an open communication line with your upper level managers is great and learning to not take too many things personally.

When asked about ways of coping with personally-directed bullying, participant RN12 stated:

For me personally, I feel like if you need to speak to someone else about the situation, I try to do that in a manner where I'm not talking bad about the person or talking behind their back. In a manner in which I can say, "Hey, I need clarification on this issue. How can I handle it?" So, it's almost more of a counselor as opposed to gossiping or talking bad because I think that makes the situation worse.

Detailed analysis of all responses pertaining to RQ2 revealed two major themes: Moral and ethical metrics (discussed by 13 of the 14 participants) and intercommunication (mentioned by all participants).

All participating nurses concurred that civility goes beyond teaching staff how to act professionally in the workplace, and is exhibited through willingness to choose to do right concerning peers. Thirteen of the interviewed nurses viewed civility as a path toward greater self and social-awareness and a means for gaining a greater appreciation for the differences in others. In practice, they felt civility was also demonstrated by consciously practicing self-control and recognizing the role each party played in any bullying incident.

ॐ

Research Question 3

What is the perceived influence on patient safety of workplace training on bullying in inpatient hospital settings? This question was addressed in individual interviews by asking the participants to respond to only one question:

How has workplace training on bullying influenced your ability to maintain standards regarding patient safety?

The findings yielded by the thematic analysis of their responses are summarized in Table 3 and are supported by some excerpts from individual interviews with the nurses.

Table 3
Benefits of anti-bullying training Received

Major themes related to specific benefits of training received	N	%
Patient safety and welfare	14	100

When asked to comment on the direct benefits of workplace training aimed at eradication of bullying on nurses' performance and patient safety, I received the following responses. Participant RN06 explained that the main challenge in eliminating bullying behaviors from hospitals stems from patients often mimicking disruptive behaviors of health care staff that can potentially affect patient safety.

RN06 said, "You also try and keep the other patients from triggering this behavior."

RN03 said the following:

I will say, because of where I work, and because of the training and stuff, I'm not afraid to go up to a doctor and say, "Hey, did you forget this, or did you mean to order this?" Most of the time the doctors are like, "Oh my God, thanks."

The response by RN03 suggested that both training and nurses' self-confidence play a role in their ability to take control of situations that could potentially escalate to more serious issues. Younger nurses may be more affected by bullying because they don't have as much experience to draw upon.

RN01 discussed benefits of workplace anti-bullying training offered in the current organization by referring to a situation in which a peer offered support when this participant was being bullied by a supervisor. RN01 indicated that the extent of the disagreement potentially created an environment that could have affected patient safety. In the words of RN01:

Another nurse even went to my superior because this one person —team leader—was bullying me. I just remember it being very heated, but that lady was very, I mean she was just really condescending to everything I was doing in the room, but the person was crashing, so it delays care. It delays your ability to think critically. It's almost like someone's stabbing you and you're trying to provide care to someone else. Afterwards, I did talk to her about it, but during the moment, I remember one of the nurses saying, "Let's focus on the patient." That kind of helped me get my mind back in to it, and it kind of redirected her behavior.

RN04 shared a much more positive experience of working on the unit:

Um, I would say that we are more like a family. And it makes the patient safer because the nurses feel, because they're supported, they feel that they are able to go to anyone at any point in time. When it comes to patient safety, this creates a better environment of safety when the nurses feel like no question is a stupid question.

RN14 shared that "anything that distracts a nurse doing her job jeopardizes that skill level of that nurse." RN14 justified the comment about jeopardizing skills by referring to an incident of witnessing a younger colleague being bullied by a seasoned nurse. RN14 shared positive perceptions of the manner in which a younger nurse dealt with a clearly uncomfortable situation, noting that "the younger nurse was a better nurse because she walked in and treated those patients as if they belonged to her."

All 14 registered nurses expressed that they use personal reasoning when trying to ensure patient safety and wellbeing.

Moreover, they regularly involve nursing leadership or peers in their decisions pertaining to ethical conduct and addressing bullying behaviors.

Analysis of their responses to RQ3 revealed two major themes that were discussed by all 14 interviewees: Patient safety and welfare, and leadership support.

All participants expressed difficulty in safeguarding patients' wellbeing without the support of nursing leadership and peers. Although they concurred that the training received did not prepare them for their clinical practice, the training did prompt them to seek support from their colleagues, thereby implicitly promoting a more positive work environment and increasing their self-confidence in their ability to fulfill their duties.

Research Question 4

In order to answer RQ4 "What do RNs perceive that inpatient hospitals can do to improve workplace training on bullying?" the interviewees were asked to respond to the following questions:

- What do you think would improve workplace training for nurses to help reduce future bullying?
- What other comments would you would like to share regarding bullying and workplace training?

Thirteen of the study participants voiced concern with the quality of the training offered and the absence of official channels for reporting bullying. These interview questions were expected to elicit a wide range of suggestions and recommendations for improvements. The participants drew upon their personal experiences with both training and workplace bullying to confirm the presence of a great disparity between theory and practice. The respondents offered many alternatives to the current training format which they deemed ineffective and in many cases counterproductive. Analysis of their responses revealed several major themes that coalesced around disciplinary consequences and barriers of education/training.

Disciplinary consequences are an organizational issue, but a process must be established to ensure that employees at all levels of an organization are accountable for their actions and decisions. According to the participants, accountability may include employee representation on important hospital committees and within-agency decision-making groups. The key findings pertaining to this question are summarized in Table 4 and are supplemented with quotes that exemplify the topics discussed on the issues of workplace obstacles and barriers to better utilization of education and training aimed at eradicating bullying from hospitals.

Table 4

Obstacles to Bullying Prevention

Major themes related to obstacles to bullying prevention	N	%
Disciplinary consequences	13	93

When the acute care nurses were asked to share their perceptions of workplace anti-bullying training presently offered in their organizations, only one offered positive views whereas, 13 of the 14 referred to the lack of consequences for inappropriate behaviors as the main hindrance to the success of any anti-bullying initiatives.

RN09 opined:

I think having an unbiased dedicated person in a high-ranking position that they could talk to or submit written anonymous problems. A lot of the times people don't report because they don't feel like they're going to be heard or they're going to be punished for reporting. To let each other know they're doing a good job instead of constantly pointing out where they're not doing a good job. Positive reinforcement.

When asked to propose ways to improve the current format of the workplace anti-bullying training, RN07 suggested the following:

You should have different conferences or maybe women across the nation who have experienced this. Have them talk maybe once a month and have that be something that's a constant model for the floors, or maybe every other month. It should never be that it's just once a month or once every summer or whatever. It should be something that's always a constant model.

RN07 elaborated on ways to improve training, and noted the following:

It [training] needs to be a continuous effort. Just being exposed to that was an eye opener for me. Even though I haven't been exposed to it, I was close to it because I was very close to the young lady and it [escalated] to a point where she almost lost her job. I think if it's a continuous effort, I think that it should be an awareness for every nurse whether in Med Surge or not. It should be something that is continuously talked about.

Participants' comments about ways to reduce bullying incidents indicated a shared perception among nurses that having bullying publicized and discussed in more open forums would increase the confidence of victims and witnesses to report bullying, or even encourage them to challenge the perpetrator directly. Given that there is a misguided perception that bullying is an integral part of health care profession, changing this narrative would also eradicate this erroneous view of the stresses that nurses have to endure as a part of their role.

RN05 indicated that bullying could be multifaceted and expressed the following:

> They need to have a day or two days of straight up bullying and all of that you're talking about. I think they need to have that in a course and teach that. Bullying, people have one perception of what basically bullying is, but the way you're putting it, it's several different things.

RN05 recommended the following:

> There needs to be some form of a consequence behind bullying, like they're not going to take this bullying lightly or whatever goes with that lightly. They have to put their foot down as far as the first time you get a written warning. What is that where they say that they just talk to you but it's not written down or anything?

The examples indicate that nurses report more confidence in the effectiveness of practical actions, rather than mere discussions about bullying that have no benefits for the victims or consequences for the perpetrators.

RN03 concurred that the main tool in bullying prevention involves the following points:

> Consequences for their actions, because I don't think there's a lot of that for nurses. The lead nurses go to training on how to deal with this and deal with that. They don't offer it as much to the line nurses, the floor nurses. I think sometimes older nurses think that new nurses are supposed to know everything, and they forget that

they're fresh out of school or whatever, and that they don't know as much. I think that they should notice who can coddle that person. Not coddle them, but be more attentive to their needs. We had some new nurses quit because their trainers were so rude to them. Department had a small little meeting every six months or whatever, and someone who was very articulate and vivacious that could get people interested in listening to them, and telling them about workplace bullying. Because sometimes you go to meetings and you tune out.

RN03's comments provide an example of the importance of practical support for nurses. This support can take many forms, but is primarily offered by peers, as the nursing profession is team based. RN01 indicated that training would be more successful if better defined and aligned with the specific needs of individual nurses.

RN01 noted the following:

I think if it was clearly defined for, especially new nurses coming, and old nurses, that would be good. Then, two, giving nurses the knowledge of what they can do, like a plan of action of what they can do to both report it and know that it's going to be helped. The tools you can use in grade school aren't necessarily what you can use in adult world, so we need better tools. We can't stop and run away, or turn away and walk away. We can't do that when you're providing patient care. It would be abandonment. I don't know that the education that's provided for nurses is giving them the tools that they need to deal with childish immature. We have nurses, you know, that are abusive.

RN01's assertion about the need for better tools for adults is aligned with the literature review, which revealed that most extant studies on bullying were conducted in school context, thus limiting the potential for transferability of the suggestions and recommendations.

RN08 was also an avid supporter of greater consequences for bullying actions. RN08 asserted that "they have to have that consequence, if that makes sense? I see it, but once you get to the consequence level, then they're willing to take a step back and say, Okay, I'll stop."

RN12 suggested that involving leadership in the training is important, because workplace initiatives can only be successful if they are fully embraced by superiors who also model the behaviors taught in the training.

RN12 responded:

First off, they need to be present within the environment and act as role models, influence those around them with a positive attitude, making sure they're not talking about other employees, about their faults or about those who have weaker skills. Just not talking bad about the employees, so really just being good role models is what the leadership needs to do.

RN14 recommended that the workplace anti-bullying training be offered as a separate program, rather than being part of a broader initiative, such as codes of conduct. In the interview, RN14 responded, "I think that what you have taken on is a specific topic but I think it's equal to everything else. I've made that clear in our conversations."

In relation to RQ4, registered nurses shared their perceptions and experience concerning workplace anti-bullying training and discussed how the training benefited in their nursing practice. Analysis of their responses revealed two major themes discussed by 13 of the participants: Disciplinary consequences and barriers of education and training.

Additional Findings

Although the findings presented in the preceding sections are based on the responses that were discussed by a majority of the interviewees, additional findings arose during the individual telephone interviews that may be important to nursing leadership. Several participants mentioned additional topics that are particularly valuable for increasing the understanding of nurses' perceptions of workplace anti-bullying training experiences.

Although all interviewees responded to a set of predefined questions, they were also prompted to explore topics further as they so chose. Additional prompting elicited valuable informal conversations, during which the participants revealed their self-awareness of their own role in bullying, the damaging effects of being forced to work in fear and the expectations of nursing leadership. Recognizing one's role in a bullying situation is the key factor in mitigating bullying behaviors. Whether one is a victim or a bully, both parties contribute to the perpetuation of harmful acts, and recognizing this is the first step toward resolving workplace bullying issues.

The additional findings are summarized in Table 5 and are supplemented with quotes that exemplify the topics discussed on the issues of fear in the workplace, and leadership training aimed at eradicating bullying from hospitals.

Table 5

Workplace Fear and Bullying Leadership Training

Other themes related to workplace bullying	N	%
Fear in the workplace	10	71
Leadership training	13	93

The discussion on working in fear elicited the following observation from RN12 about leadership: "I feel that she rules with fear." This assertion is indicative that allowing nurse leaders to instill fear in their subordinates perpetuates a culture of fear within the units in the hospital and increases the likelihood of mistakes being made, thus compromising patient safety.

RN12 noted:

My nurse leader always puts on a good face while walking the halls and smiling and asking everyone how their day was, which is great. However, when a situation arises, you see her act harshly and cruelly to the extent of writing people up unnecessarily and almost to the point of firing, you know? She walks around with a big stick.

RN07 was of the view that, rather than harboring resentment and fear, nurses should talk about issues. RN07 noted that, when working with more senior colleagues, young nurses often defer to them for guidance, which may perpetuate fear of their own incompetence. In reference to one such incident, RN07 explained, "I think she knew what to do. I think she was just afraid." RN04 exhibited high levels of self-confidence and assertiveness and shared, "I'm not going to allow you to half do this or half say that or behave in this manner just because I'm afraid of you or because that person may be afraid of you."

As exemplified by excerpts of participant interview responses, the feelings regarding fear of the leadership and of speaking up were mixed among the study participants. Participants who spoke of feeling fearful of mistreatment by leadership stated that this sense of powerlessness hindered their ability to fight against the bullying leaders. One-half of the participants were rather confident in their ability to assert themselves whereas the other one-half spoke of a lack of confidence to speak up and fear of their direct superiors.

Ten of the nurses interviewed seemed to feel apprehensive about their direct leaders. It was appropriate to ask them to share their perceptions of nursing leadership expectations on when workplace anti-bullying training was particularly relevant, given the lack of anti-bullying policies in the health care organizations they worked for. RN03 shared the following: "Well, to me it needs to start in school. Because I don't think there's a lot of training on that in school."

RN01 was of a different view and noted:

> I think it starts with management. Mainly because this is my own situation, but training for those people that are going into team leader or management positions. It can't be the same training for the nurses it is for the manager. You know, because there's people sometimes that think if the word isn't completely defined well, like it is in the public school system.

RN09 felt that nurses should be given more extensive training, as well as support by their leaders. RN09 stated, "If the right training had been out there, maybe we wouldn't know the term [going postal]."

All 14 participants felt that more should be done at the organizational level to assist nurses in performing their jobs to their maximum potential. Nurses work under extensive pressure that should not be exacerbated by inadequate leadership and lack of support. In particular, if those persons in nursing leadership positions are not given workplace anti-bullying training, inappropriate behavior will perpetuate and will never be eradicated from hospitals.

⟡

CHAPTER FOUR SUMMARY

This chapter includes discussion of the findings yielded by a thematic analysis of individual telephone interviews held with 14 acute care nurses in the Oklahoma City metropolitan area.

The chapter commences with a brief overview of the pilot study and demographic analysis of participants' characteristics. The overview is followed by the presentation of findings, which are aligned with the four research questions that guided the study.

Thematic analysis of interview transcripts revealed many useful topics from which nurse leaders can benefit. Five themes are of particular relevance for the future emerged from the data analysis.

- Ineffectiveness of Workplace anti-bullying training
- Coping Strategies Employed by Nurses
- Benefits of anti-bullying training Received
- Obstacles to Bullying Prevention
- Workplace Fear and Bullying Leadership Training

The dissertation concludes with Chapter Five, whereby the study findings presented are interpreted in light of the extant literature on the subject. The interpretation is followed by the study implications for research and practice, limitations, researcher reflections, recommendations for practice, recommendation for future research and a conclusion of the study.

Chapter Four Notes

_____
_____
_____
_____
_____
_____
_____
_____
_____
_____
_____
_____
_____
_____
_____
_____
_____
_____
_____
_____
_____
_____
_____
_____
_____
_____
_____
_____
_____
_____

CHAPTER FIVE

CONCLUSIONS AND RECOMMENDATIONS

*E*ffective workplace training aimed at preventing bullying is essential for hospitals, as any incidents of inappropriate or threatening behavior may compromise not only staff effectiveness, but also patient safety. The bullying issue is widely recognized in the health care arena. Hospital leadership has difficulties implementing the requisite changes.

An exploration of the effectiveness of workplace anti-bullying training is necessary, as the findings yielded could assist hospital leaders in developing appropriate anti-bullying strategies. Educating leaders how to recognize fear, intimidation and retaliation among victims and bullies is suggested to improve anti-bullying strategies in health care organizations.

Thematic analysis of participant narratives confirmed that nursing leaders are aware of bullying behaviors in their units, yet many leaders fail to address bullying effectively. In particular, the study results indicated that leaders tend to become complacent when monitoring the outcomes of workplace anti-bullying training programs. Thematic analysis clearly confirms that offering training as a stand-alone measure is insufficient in eliminating bullying from hospitals. Additional strategies need to be considered to ensure that appropriate training is implemented correctly and is offered to all staff members.

In addition to monitoring attendance, human resource managers should also enforce polices designed to mitigate workplace bullying and penalizing perpetrators. It is crucial to provide a means of reporting bullying incidents, emphasizing that such behaviors should not be perceived as an integral part of the nursing job.

The literature review conducted as a part of this investigation revealed a gap in extant knowledge regarding the effects of not having a clear, effective and consistent method for the development or implementation of bullying prevention strategies on the performance of health care organizations and safety of their staff and patients. In particular, few extant studies have assessed the effectiveness of workplace anti-bullying training programs in health care settings. While ample research exists regarding bullying and prevention strategies in other organizations (particularly schools), the findings cannot be generalized to hospital settings because of the individualized effect of bullying behavior when considering victim age and other variables.

The stressful environment in which health care practitioners work may make effective situational communication difficult. If left unaddressed, bullying can have not only have damaging effects on the affected individuals, but the entire team and the institution as a whole. Bullying behaviors can compromise patient safety and must be eradicated from hospital units.

Establishing workplace anti-bullying training programs in hospitals can be challenging because of employee work schedules and rapidly changing work teams that may hinder implementation of the learned tools and strategies. Hospital leadership must specify concrete disciplinary actions for bullying behaviors. Improvements to the existing workplace anti-bullying programs should be made to make them more relevant to nursing practice, and attendance should be mandatory. Implementation of the learned content should be evaluated periodically and any changes made if necessary.

Given the gap in extant literature, the purpose of this qualitative exploratory study was to explore workplace training that nurses received regarding bullying, nurses' perceptions regarding the effectiveness of that training and their ability to cope with bullying. In addition, they were prompted to offer suggestions regarding improvements that could be made to make training more effective in preventing bullying in hospitals.

Ensuring patient safety while offering high quality care is the ultimate goal of the health care profession. Nurses' perceptions regarding how bullying impacts their ability to care for patients as well as how it may compromise patient safety was explored. To meet study objectives a qualitative approach was adopted, whereby the experiences of 14 acute care nurses in Oklahoma City metropolitan area hospitals were sought via telephone interviews.

଼

IMPLICATION OF FINDINGS

The goal of this exploratory qualitative inquiry was to examine the perceptions of acute care nurses regarding the effectiveness of workplace anti-bullying training. In addition, participants were prompted to discuss their ability to cope with bullying they encounter as a part of their role. They were given the opportunity to offer suggestions for improvements in the workplace anti-bullying training they currently receive. Participants were also asked to share their views regarding the effects bullying has on patient safety and on their ability to do their jobs.

The following discussion of the results pertaining to each research question is based on the more detailed findings presented in Chapter Four and is accompanied by excerpts of participant responses to support the claims made.

ॐ

Research Question 1

RQ1 asked, "How have workplace training programs influenced the ability, or inability, of RNs to respond to bullying in inpatient hospital settings?"

The participants voiced their dissatisfaction with the quality and the curriculum design of the workplace anti-bullying training currently offered in their units. They were of the view that the ineffectiveness of the workplace anti-bullying training had compromised the practical significance of the education received, because the participants did not acquire sufficient ability to predict or prevent bullying behaviors.

Analysis of participants' feedback related to RQ1 revealed three major themes:

- Lack of uniformity among training programs,
- Lack of resources for workplace bullying prevention
- Limitations regarding the availability of training.

Establishment of standardization of workplace anti-bullying training and providing nurses with effective tools should be expected. According to Sheridan's[42] study findings, providing nursing staff with an effective training program that focuses on strategies for managing aggression has a positive affect on their ability to address bullying behaviors in the workplace. Limited opportunities for attending anti-bullying training programs that incorporate strategies for managing aggression and inappropriate behaviors affect not only the nursing staff but the entire organization.[42] Nurses perceive insufficient training as a major barrier to their ability to appropriately respond to bullying incidents.[138] This shortcoming was addressed in the present study, where the effectiveness of such programs was explored through the perspectives of nurse participants.

A consensus among participants identified that the lack of consistency of information and presentation (e.g., individualized in-services or computerized testing), of the anti-bullying training was counterproductive within the nursing learning environment. As agreed among 13 participants, the lack of resources with the training is linked to increased potential for individuals to experience bullying in the nursing practice or to fail to develop the tools needed to fight against bullying. The interpretation of limitations regarding availability of workplace anti-bullying training provided by the participants suggested that the training lacks the importance of other training provided within the organization. All 14 participants were able to recall participating in some form of workplace anti-bullying training and were thus prompted to discuss these experiences when answering the interview questions.

Sheridan,[42] Simon and Sauer[123] and Strandmark and Rahm[139] conducted studies in order to examine anti-bullying training programs presently offered in the health care industry. Their findings confirm that effective training programs help increase nurses' knowledge of this prevalent phenomenon, as well as equip them with the skills required to manage aggression or bullying behaviors in the workplace proactively.

The authors who have conducted studies seeking employees'

views of the effectiveness of anti-bullying training programs reported that most of these initiatives failed to enhance the employees' skills or provide strategies that could be implemented to combat bullying.[125,138] On the other hand, in an earlier study conducted by Sheridan,[42] even though the participants became more aware of their environment, they had very few resources at their disposal because the course content and delivery mode was determined by the leadership.

This was supported by the present study findings, as 13 participants were of view that the workplace anti-bullying training they received was ineffective because they were not given the necessary resources to confront bullying acts. Moreover, the curriculum did not include interpersonal skills techniques they could adopt to address inappropriate behaviors in a non-hostile manner. However, Livington et al.,[125] and Quinlan et al.[138] also noted the scarcity of research on staff training. In their view, the training offered to nurses tends to have a very limited scope, comprised of intervention, reporting and discussion of bullying occurrences in the health care organization.

Thus, in recognition of the outdated format of most training programs currently in use, the Washington State Department of Labor and Industries[145] stipulated that de-escalation training be used to deal with bullying interaction. As a part of such training programs, nurses should be encouraged to share their experiences and discuss strategies that should be adopted in such cases in order to prevent bullying incidents from escalating into serious issues affecting staff morale, productivity and thus patient safety.

When commenting on the curriculum content, RN01 espoused, "It doesn't really give people the tools that they need to be able to deal with it when it's happening." The participant went on to say that, "I don't think that it really—I think it's only brought awareness, but not prevention."

RN12 offered similar view, "I would say there's no benefits to the training other than it checks a box off, and I can continue on and it doesn't require a lot of effort on our part."

RN03 referred to the anti-bullying training experience in equally unfavorable terms, stating, "Well one thing is, it's the same one every year, so you kind of memorize it, so it's meaningless."

RN11 noted, "It's not really a training tool. We just kind of whiz through it, just to check them off. It's not very effective training." RN11 was particularly critical of the computerized training modules, which was described as, "kind of a joke."

The participants' views concur with the findings yielded by extant research. For example, Simon and Sauer[123] posited that basic anti-bullying training must include discussion on how health care professionals should respond when confronted with bullying behaviors. In addition, participants were unanimous in their assertion that, if hospitals improved the workplace anti-bullying training and offered it to all employees, bullying behaviors could be quickly resolved. Yet, RN12 was not convinced that hospital management could make such positive changes and noted, "I don't think there needs to be more because I don't feel that the training we get is any good, so why throw more bad training at the situation."

According to the findings yielded by the literature review, the primary aim of the Healthy Workplace Bill[170] is introducing the conflict resolution approach into the training programs. This enhancement will assist nurses in becoming team players, thus allowing them to influence each other in decision-making strategies in a productive, respectful and appropriate manner. In order to alleviate the ongoing bullying problem, the human resources department and nursing leadership could jointly determine policies that all employees must abide by. This joint effort will increase the likelihood that the nursing staff will adhere to the workplace conduct standards that have zero tolerance for bullying.[6,13]

Research Question 2

RQ2 asked, "What is the perceived influence on job performance in inpatient hospital settings of workplace training on bullying?"

When discussing this topic, most surveyed nurses noted that, as the workplace anti-bullying training they received was ineffective, it had very little practical influence. In the participants' view, workplace anti-bullying training has an indirect effect on job performance, exerted through internal self-controlling strategies such as promoting ethical behaviors. The finding about anti-bullying training increasing internal control is consistent with the literature, as according to Ashker et al.[135] and Stagg, Sheridan, Jones and Speroni,[170] having multiple plans, and some form of self-controlling strategy applied to workplace anti-bullying training, deters bullying acts within the everyday work environment.

All participants indicated they have used some form of self-control to resolve bullying acts and improve their job performance, which could be seen as a benefit of the training they received. Purpora, Blegen and Stotts[172] explored the relationship between nurses' beliefs about themselves and their reflections on bullying acts in hospital and other health care settings. Oore et al.[119] suggested civility as a particularly useful self-controlling intervention, as they found it effective in increasing individuals' ability to cope with stress-related issues at work. Civility is a person-focused approach that promotes strong relationships among co-workers and positive outcomes.[130,119,117]

Analysis of participant responses pertaining to RQ2 revealed findings congruent with the assertions made by Ashker et al.[135] and Oore et al.[119] Two themes emerged from thematic analysis: Use of personal moral and ethical standards and interpersonal communication. The participants reported that personal morality and ethics (13 of 14 participants) and interpersonal communication (14 participants) had the capability to create a work environment relatively safe from bullying by colleagues, no matter the professional level of the person being bullied.

Individuals' morale may improve by understanding, identifying bullying behaviors and addressing negative interpersonal communication within the work environment.[121,122,29] Ethics and morality equip individuals to do what is right.[29] Participants internalized the lack of positive interpersonal communication, ethics and morals as uncivil behavior that is often associated with a loss of power in the nursing professional. Whether nurses perceived bullying acts as intentional or unintentional, a decrease in interpersonal communication reduced perceived levels of morale among the participants.

Thirteen participants concurred that civility goes beyond teaching nurses how to act professionally in the workplace, and that civility is exhibited through willingness to choose to do right in regard to peers. Thirteen of the interviewed nurses viewed civility as a path toward greater self and social-awareness, and a means for gaining a greater appreciation of differences in others. In practice, they felt civility was also demonstrated by consciously practicing self-control and recognizing the part each person played in any bullying incident.

For instance, participant RN14 responded: "You just know better. I won't tolerate it in any way on my watch any more than I will tolerate race discrimination because of who I am at a heart/soul level, not because of my training. I function based on a moral compass, not an educational level."

Similarly, RN08 stated, "Well, the best thing you can do is to just remain calm and to not take it personal, because the thing about bullying is that it's about the other person, it has nothing to do with you."

Participant RN01 said, "Because of the training module, it

made me more aware of it and I think the nurses are kind of left to themselves to find coping strategies. I just try to slow my breathing down; I try to listen. When I respond, I talk a lot slower. It helps me to be more calm. Then it kind of slows down, or I say nothing, and/or try to get away from the situation."

Participant RN03 acknowledged that the training improved her job performance and shared the following: "I think I speak up a little bit more now. Not that I've always been a quiet person, but I think I've learned to tell the person immediately, 'Hey, that really upset me.'"

RN09 recommended, "Going back to the whole respect factor and put yourself in somebody else's place. How would you want to be treated? I think a lot of it is being able to talk with your co-workers, developing that bond where you can let it all out, deescalate yourself."

In response related to RQ2, participant RN11 recalled giving a "personal in-service to my own unit about bullying. I wanted to at least try to take that information back to my peers. I also became a personal mentor to one of our newer nurses." As can be seen from these excerpts, 13 study participants felt that choosing to do right for the other person was a way to prevent recurrences of bullying. All 14 participants relied on interpersonal communication as their primary coping strategy to help create a work environment free of bullying.

Wright[141] confirmed that the aforementioned strategies are effective, based on the finding that health care workers with better communication skills are less likely to encounter repeated bullying acts.

RN08 supported Wright's[141] statement by stating: "If you do debrief, debriefings probably about the best thing because they can say 'Well hey I noticed this' or 'They told me that.' And so that once we share that and we allow them to share their stories. In sharing that with purpose. Sharing that with purpose, not as for making them feel belittled or anything like that."

When commenting on the effects of bullying on her self-esteem, RN11 espoused, "I don't get overly upset about it being a bullying situation. Those are other people's actions. I've learned to have an open communication line with your upper level managers is great and learning to not take too many things personally." Participant RN12 offered a similar perspective to RN11, "For me personally, I feel like if you need to speak to someone else about the situation. I try to do that in a manner where I'm not talking bad about the person or talking behind their back."

છ

Research Question 3

RQ3 asked, "What is the perceived influence on patient safety of workplace training on bullying in inpatient hospital settings?"

This question was answered as a part of the present study as, according to Laschinger,[49] lack of communication among physicians, nurses and other team members can have unfavorable effects on the patients and may even jeopardize patients' safety. An exploratory study conducted by Berry et al.[46] revealed that 77% of the participants reported being targets of repeated bullying, which compromised their productivity. Moreover, their assertions confirmed that workplace bullying is problematic for health care organizations. Failure to adequately address workplace bullying may result in nurses leaving their job or even the profession, thus creating staff shortages and potentially endangering patients.

The dire consequences of workplace bullying in the health care sector should encourage other researchers to explore the bullying issue further, with the goal of proposing effective anti-bullying strategies.[75] Once productivity and willingness to perform one's duties are compromised, the quality of care the patients receive is also brought into question, thus endangering the entire organization and the health care system as a whole[114,46,25,62]

When participant responses related to this research question were analyzed, patient safety and welfare and leadership emerged as the two main themes. All 14 participants expressed that they were conscious of the effects of bullying on patient care and welfare and had some level of leadership support in combating this issue.

For example, RN03 posited, "I will say, because of where I work, and because of the training and stuff, I'm not afraid to go up to a doctor and say, 'Hey, did you forget this, or did you mean to order this?' Most of the time the doctors are like, "Oh my God, thanks."

When discussing effects of bullying on patient safety, participant RN06 explained that the issue is exacerbated when patients mimic disruptive behaviors exhibited by health care staff. RN06 shared that, in order to mitigate this effect, an effort is made to identify triggers for such disruptive behaviors. RN06 went on to say, "You also try and keep the other patients from triggering this behavior."

In responding to this question, RN01 recalled being offered support by a peer when being bullied by a supervisor, which potentially created an environment that compromised patient safety. RN01 recalled, "I remember one of the nurses saying, 'let's focus on the patient.' That kind of helped me get my mind back in to it, and it kind of redirected her behavior."

RN04, on the other hand, observed, "Um, I would say that we are more like a family. And it makes the patient safer because the nurses feel, because they're supported, they feel that they are able to go to anyone at any point in time."

RN14 shared, "Anything that distracts a nurse [from] doing her job jeopardizes that skill level of that nurse."

Research Question 4

RQ4 asked the following: "What do RNs perceive that inpatient hospitals can do to improve workplace training on bullying?"

This question related to the prevalent view that leaders should be the voices for both patients and nurses and should be held accountable for the activities taking place within the unit. When interpersonal interactions are unproductive and unprofessional nurses resort to aggressive and bullying behaviors, the leaders should be held accountable, because they should serve as role models for their staff and are responsible for addressing any issues among the team members. Failure to do so results in employees developing negative perceptions of their leaders.[58,65]

Leymann[58] further noted that leaders should also take the initiative in addressing bullying incidents by confronting the responsible individual and implementing appropriate disciplinary measures. However, for leaders to be effective and accountable, they must focus on developing effective communication skills that includes active listening skills.

According to the report issued by the Baldridge Performance Excellence Program,[173] employing a leadership system program should be viewed as a systemic approach to creating a successful health care organization and ensuring ongoing improvement. In particular, leaders must be aware of the key elements of setting directions and ensure that all employees are given access to the necessary training and development programs, such as workplace anti-bullying prevention initiatives.[173] When employers fail to respond to bullying incidents that members of staff report, civil rights acts may sanction legal actions to protect the affected individuals from bullying.[174,185,66,65]

Baum[176] concurred with this view, further noting that, in the absence of legal consequences, leaders can take action to support a healthier workplace and alleviate the potential for bullying to occur. The BPEP[173] recommended 6 approaches that could be effective in combating bullying:

- Evaluate leadership style of management,
- Plan individual or group educational activities that focus on defining bullying,
- Enforce a no-bullying policy,
- Use conflict resolution/effective communication after reporting an incident,
- Use critical thinking skills when employing potential employees, and
- Place reminder posters throughout the workplace.

Analysis of participant responses pertaining to RQ4 revealed two common themes: Disciplinary consequences and barriers of education and training. All participants recommended that hospitals enforce consequences and redesign the teaching methods.

For example, participant RN08 believes that that the organization needs to hold nurses accountable to the rules. RN08 noted: "The thing is that, once everybody understands that there's accountability for the type of behavior. Because out of that training, there will be a cost if you want to come to work and bully people. You won't work there anymore, so people know there's a consequence. If sometimes when you give a consequence, it kind of curtails their behavior a little bit. I'm just saying there is rules. We just set the limit. We just set the standard."

RN03 concurred with this view, asserting that nurses who bully their colleagues need, "consequences for their actions, because I don't think there's a lot of that for nurses." The participant added, "The lead nurses go to training on how to deal with this and deal with that."

RN03 suggested that the training should be provided by,

"someone who was very articulate and vivacious that could get people interested in listening to them, and telling them about workplace bullying. Because sometimes you go to meetings and you tune out."

RN01 shared, "I think if it was clearly defined for especially new nurses coming and old nurses that would be good. Then, two, giving nurses the knowledge of what they can do, like a plan of action of what they can do to both report it and know that it's going to be helped." In addition, RN01 suggested changes to the resources provided to nurses, stating, "Tools you can use in grade school aren't necessarily what you can use in adult world, so we need better tools."

RN08 believed that "they have to have that consequence, if that makes sense? I see it, but once you get to the consequence level, then they're willing to take a step back and say, 'Okay, I'll stop.'"

RN12 felt that involving leadership in the training is important, offering the following recommendations: "First off, they need to be present within the environment and act as role models, influence those around them with a positive attitude, making sure they're not talking about other employees." RN14 commented how the workplace anti-bullying training should be designed and be included as a separate program. RN14 stated, "I think that what you have taken on is a specific topic but I think it's equal to everything else."

The inadequacy of an existing workplace anti-bullying policy makes it very difficult to use punitive actions in practice. This, in turn, is likely to escalate bullying behaviors, as employees have no incentives to report these harmful acts, as they have no confidence that they would be addressed effectively by the management.[67,70,65] Hospital leadership must specify concrete disciplinary actions for bullying behaviors. In addition, improvements to the existing workplace anti-bullying programs should be made to make them more relevant to nursing practice, while making attendance mandatory. Implementation of the learned content should be evaluated periodically and any changes made if necessary.

ॐ

INTERPRETATION OF THEMES

Theme 1: Ineffectiveness of Workplace Anti-bullying Training

The interpretation of Theme 1 was based on the research participants' experiences and attitudes towards specific workplace anti-bullying training they had received in the past. According to Laszlo and Krippner's[44] general system theory, system is defined as "a group of interacting components that conserves some identifiable set of relations with the sum of the components plus their relations (i.e., the system itself) conserving some identifiable set of relations to other entities (including other systems)."

In the present study, the system concept was applied to the workplace anti-bullying training and nurses' behaviors associated with bullying. The system (hospital) has apparently failed nurses, as they were under stress and felt frustrated by the fact that they were not supported in their attempts to deal with bullying. As a result, many developed inappropriate coping mechanisms to survive in their own work environment. Health care professionals, such as nurses, are not adequately equipped to address inappropriate behaviors directed towards them proactively, and often resort to retaliation.[123] Hence, they require training and guidance, as well as support by management, in order to develop strategies that would allow them to respond to bullying in an appropriate manner.

Nurses' need for strategy development training is supported by Simon and Sauer,[23] who found that most individuals who experience more frequent or more severe forms of bullying have not received effective training and lack the resources needed to confront bullying acts and the perpetrators constructively.

When discussing bullying acts directed at them, the nurses shared that these tended to be verbal. However, the anti-bullying training they had received did not improve their ability to confront the perpetrator or resolve the situation. The participants found this rather frustrating. For example, RN14 shared that the training was "very annoying" as it did not influence people's attitudes towards others.

On the other hand, RN01 described the anti-bullying training as a "continuing education credit, and then it doesn't really give people the tools that they need to be able to deal with it when it's happening." One may infer from this view that training was provided primarily as a means of ensuring that nurses were pursuing further education, rather than aiming to assist them with practical issues they faced in the workplace. This is in line with the assertion made by RN03, who referred to the training as "meaningless and they should make it more important."

In sum, 13 of 14 study participants suggested that the ineffectiveness of workplace anti-bullying training stemmed from the lack of uniformity and resources, as well as the limitations of the education they were offered. Analysis of participants' responses indicate that these issues related to training were further exacerbated by the lack of a consistent definition of bullying. As a result, the workplace anti-bullying training they were offered was ineffective, hindering the participants from fully understanding the magnitude and prevalence of the negative behaviors and the effects on the victims. In addition, not having a precise definition of workplace bullying made it difficult to develop and implement effective prevention and coping strategies.

Van Hulle and Marshall[177] found that recognizing and addressing bullying behaviors early is a key factor in preventing bullying acts from damaging team dynamics. According to Van Hulle and Marshall,[177] applying an effective comprehensive workplace anti-bullying training program involves four steps, denoted by the acronym RACE: Recognize, Assess, Control and Evaluate. When implemented correctly at the workplace, RACE bullying-prevention training enables organizational leaders to define, identify and prevent bullying from occurring, resulting in a transparent and accountable environment.

Perceptions of the ineffectiveness of workplace anti-bullying training are necessarily subjective; they must be addressed. The process can start by removing the barriers for the implementation of training programs such as RACE, which may ultimately have a positive effect on patient safety, and improve employees' performance.[143] However, organizational leaders must be aware that there is no quick fix, nor a one-size-fits-all solution.[143] Each organization is unique and faces different challenges. Still, proportionate actions and non-judgmental support are the key ingredients of an effective training environment.

Theme 2: Coping Strategies Employed by Nurses

Theme 2 was derived from the participants' thoughts, comments and perceptions related to the coping strategies they used in dealing with workplace bullying. When considering the conceptual framework ideas, which helped drive this study, general system theory developed by Laszlo and Krippner[44] provided valuable insight into specific components that affect the functioning of the whole (training), and each individual unit (nurse), as all components are interrelated and are thus affected by at least one other component in the system.

Working collaboratively is essential for organizations to function and create a healthy working culture that is supportive and inclusive of all staff.[137] If nurses do not receive training, a part of which is learning effective anti-bullying strategies, they may develop coping skills that are neither effective nor equip them for dealing with future occurrences of bullying in the workplace.[42]

As most study participants found workplace anti-bullying training ineffective, they sought alternative coping strategies to deal with bullying. Although each individual was affected by harmful behaviors of others differently, all 14 participants specifically referred to reliance on a moral code and ethics as an effective coping strategy. Elaborating further, most nurses stated that they relied on interpersonal communication with friends, colleagues and nursing leadership to share their problems because this helped them cope better with unpleasant situations.

Empirical evidence suggests that coping strategies that help individuals develop problem-solving skills, such as reliance on a moral code, ethical conduct and communication with others, have a broader affect because they usually help de-escalate bullying occurrences.[178,179] Moreover, when employees have interrelated duties that impact the performances of individuals as well as the entire team, they are more likely to be willing to address any workplace issues. According to Leon-Perez et al.,[153] for interrelated teams that work toward a common goal, problem solving is a favorable approach for addressing and ultimately eradicating workplace bullying.

For example, RN14 stated, "I function based on a moral compass, not an educational level," implying that each individual should be able to distinguish right from wrong behavior. RN08 held similar views, and observed, "We just set the standard."

On the other hand, for RN04, "Debriefing's probably about the best thing." This participant supported the premise that sharing problems with others and actively participating in addressing them can mitigate the harmful effects of bullying.

This view was shared by RN11 who indicated that "I've learned to have an open communication line with your upper level managers is great." Karatuna[180] highlighted the importance of striving to find problem-focused solutions when confronting workplace bullying. However, for this strategy to be effective, both the leaders and the employees must take part in formal training that allows them to identify bullying patterns and mitigate destructive behaviors within the organization. Karatuna[180] further posited that organizations can prevent bullying by establishing an effective anti-bullying program and a formal complaint process.

Theme 3: Benefits of Anti-bullying Training Received

The interpretation of Theme 3 is aligned with the findings yielded by the literature review conducted. Von Bertalanffy[45] suggested that, from a general system point of view, the hospital is a system operating within a broader environment that determines the quality of a nurses' workplace, imposing certain expectations regarding staff conduct. As a result, attitudes, behaviors and perceptions of all nurses are intertwined and affect the performance of the system as a whole (i.e., determine the quality of the work environment).

Extant studies in the field indicate that when bullying victims or witnesses are not given leadership support the harmful effects of such acts are exacerbate. Berry et al.[46] suggested that, until leaders eliminate bullying through effective policies and training, workplace bullying will remain a serious concern in most organizations. Thobaben[13] shared the same view, noting further that, when management is aware of bullying behaviors, yet chooses to ignore the issue, the culture of bullying becomes acceptable. This limits the ability of individual nurses to respond to such acts appropriately, as they lack the necessary support and feel isolated. Moreover, ample empirical evidence suggests that nurses' bullying actions often influence the manner in which nurses approach their nursing practice. For instance, Hickson[56] stated that bullying behaviors often undermine employees' dedication toward patients, which can ultimately lead to compromising patient welfare.

Wilson and Phelps[134] reported that nurses experiencing bullying were less likely to ask for assistance from their peers and found that bullied nurses performed actions that could jeopardize patient safety. Riskin et al.[190] conducted a randomized trial on an NICU medical team to test how bullying behaviors affected performance and discovered that, when the members of the medical team were exposed to bullying behavior (rude behavior), their job performance declined.

The 14 participants concurred that bullying in many instances affects patient care negatively. However, upon receiving workplace anti-bullying training, all participants were able to identify positive effects on their workplace behaviors. Many shared that the training enhanced or added to their awareness of how to approach their nursing practice when faced with bullying behaviors.

For example, RN03 stated, "Because of the training and stuff, I'm not afraid to go up to a doctor."

Similarly, RN04 observed, "And it makes the patient safer because the nurses feel, because they're supported, they feel that they are able to go to anyone at any point in time."

RN07 declared, "Just knowing. You know when you see fire, you know what you're supposed to do."

RN09 added, "You are more cognizant about what was going on around you and the whole sensitivity training that's part of it. That's not what they called it, just to be aware."

Theme 4: Obstacles to Bullying Prevention

The research participants concurred that educational barriers and lack of disciplinary consequences were the primary reasons for the prevalence of bullying in their unit. RN05 suggested that, "A lot of the times people don't report because they don't feel like they're going to be heard or they're going to be punished for reporting."

RN05 opined that, "There needs to be some form of a consequence behind bullying." Similar sentiment was echoed by RN03, who observed that, if bullies would suffer "consequences for their actions," their attitudes might change. This view was shared by RN08, who agreed that "they have to have that consequence." RN12 concurred, but also noted that "leadership in the training is important," as having leadership support would likely encourage bullying victims and witnesses to come forward.

RN07 criticized the training format, expressing, "It should never be that it's just once a month or once every summer or whatever. It should be something that's always a constant model."

The lack of consequences and limited education had a definite effect upon the manner in which nurses often view themselves as the victim, a witness or the bully. In the absence of direct consequences for unprofessional behavior, bullies harm not only their victims, but also have the ability to create an unpleasant or uncomfortable work environment that may be detrimental to their peers or patients in their care.

In addition to establishing rules of professional conduct and specifically stating consequences for indiscretions, all 14 participating nurses were of the view that providing adequate education is an essential aspect of any workplace anti-bullying prevention strategy. The participants concurred that the onus of any workplace anti-bullying training program should be on promoting self-monitoring behavior, as this would discourage bullying behaviors. In addition, this approach would increase the potential for creating role models for nursing leadership within the entire organization or their respective units.

Nursing leaders may decrease the prevalence and severity of workplace bullying by actively engaging in any disputes that may arise. A proactive stance toward bullying behaviors would likely limit their occurrence within units.[131] Quinlan et al. [138] suggested that, for an organization (such as a hospital) to maximize the success of its operations, its management and all individuals in leadership positions must be proactive in developing staff training programs, as training increases knowledge and skills of all employees, thus improving efficiency. Program development also includes anti-bullying initiatives, which are necessary if these acts are to be eradicated from the workplace. Only individuals working in healthy and supportive environments can be effective and dedicated to their jobs.

Theme 5: Workplace Fear of Bullying

In an ideal world, a workplace environment would be a place of harmony. The reality is that the nursing profession is succumbing to social intimidation that threatens nurses' performance, compromises organizations' working standards and effectiveness and ultimately endangers patients. Vickers[84] asserted many nursing professionals have felt unsupported in their struggles with workplace bullying and have accepted such behaviors as an integral part of the fundamental structure of the nursing profession. The acceptance of negative behaviors from management and workplace bullies exacerbates the effects of bullying because they are often unreported, as nurses do not expect any changes in their situation and thus continue to suffer in isolation.

Faced with the burdens of bullying, nursing leadership is often inadequately prepared to address the problem. Unaddressed bullying behaviors breed fear, as those affected do not feel supported by their organization.[181] Nurses who have experienced workplace bullying in the past often live in fear of becoming the victim of further attacks.[182]

For instance, RN07 explained, "I think she knew what to do. I think she was just afraid." RN12 believed that leadership style of superiors could breed fear, stating, "I feel that she rules with fear." Commenting on the attitude of a direct supervisor, RN01 shared, "You see her act harshly and cruelly to the extent of writing people up unnecessarily and almost to the point of firing, you know? She walks around with a big stick."

Laszlo and Krippner[44] suggested that system theory could be applied when attempting to understand the multifaceted dimensions of sociocultural interaction. Within the context of Laszlo and Krippner's[44] work, the larger environment in which individuals operate is treated as the system, whereby all their actions affect others, and thus influence the functioning of the system as a whole.

Views expressed by the participants aligned with empirical evidence suggesting that failure of supervisors to modify their behavior and be more sympathetic to the issues of their subordinates can have detrimental effects on the workplace atmosphere.

For example, Price et al.[183] suggested that up to 15% of bullying attacks are not reported due to the fear of repercussions. Consequently, those who experience emotional turbulence in their professional and personal lives often suffer in silence, which further exacerbates the issue. Fear and silence are interrelated, as a victim who endures bullying in silence allows the perpetrator to continue with harmful acts.

Bennadi and Konekeri[142] suggested that symptoms of workplace bullying such as fear are common. In their view, victim's anxiety or fear may be reduced through workplace anti-bullying training for leadership. As leadership has an important influence in an organization, it is not surprising that leaders' attitudes toward bullying would set the tone for how such acts are perceived by others. Bennadi and Konekeri[142] emphasized that leadership communication style (word choice, tone and body language) is important in building a bullying-free workplace.

Selecting role models, improving communication and interaction skills and seeking regular and frank feedback from staff allows leaders to identify concerns and issues within the workplace and pave the road toward a positive work environment.

Theme 6: Bullying Leadership Training

During the interviews, the need for more effective leadership training was mentioned by most participants. In their view, inadequate training nursing leaders received on anti-bullying strategies compromised their ability to address the bullying concerns of their staff.

Workplace training programs are usually ineffective due to the poorly designed curriculum, lack of standardization and improper fit to the specific work setting.[125] Hospital managers who adopt programs that work in other organizations may not achieve the desired results, unless leaders consider the specific context and issues the employees face, which should be the starting point for designing training curriculum. Nursing leadership remains responsible for recognizing and eliminating bullying acts in the workplace. However, given that most health care organizations are comprised of diverse units and thus nursing teams (such as RN, LPN, CNA and NP), nursing leaders have complex duties within an organization, making the creation of a unified anti-bullying strategy challenging.

Strandmark and Rahm[139] suggested that health care organizations develop training programs focusing on practical skills and problem solving, as this would allow attendees to gain confidence in being able to respond to workplace bullying appropriately.

Thirteen research participants felt that bullying is allowed to proliferate within their units due to the lack of human resources policies and failure to train nursing leadership in the management and prevention of bullying behaviors.

For instance, RN03 shared, "Well, to me it needs to start in school. Because I don't think there's a lot of training on that in school." RN01 was of a different view and noted, "I think it starts with management." RN01 further observed, "It can't be the same training for the nurses it is for the manager," implying that nurse leaders have the primary responsibility for ensuring harmonious environment in their units.

RN09 felt that nurses should be given more extensive training, as well as support by their leaders. RN09 stated, "If the right training had been out there, maybe we wouldn't know the term [going postal]."

Most participants cited failure to train leadership on workplace bullying mitigation strategies, which should prompt urgent attention on behalf of management. Blum and Beck[27] suggested that, given the diverse nursing roles, following the groundbreaking Shared Responsibility Approach (SRA) could allow management to focus on the solution, rather than the blame. The program consists of three intervention steps:

- Meet and have a conversation with the victim,
- Offer or suggest support groups in which leadership also participates and
- Follow-up with the victim.

RECOMMENDATIONS FOR PRACTICE

Thematic analysis revealed participants' ideas about tools and resolution methods to mitigate workplace bullying. The recommendations that can be derived from the findings yielded by the present study are primarily based on the feedback the nurses provided during their individual interviews because they are in the ideal position to recognize elements of workplace anti-bullying training programs that are effective and those that require improvement. Because their perspectives were related to the training they received, they can assist nursing leadership in revising the design and content of the workplace anti-bullying training in order to increase practical utility. Moreover, because such initiatives are most effective when support is obtained from all stakeholders, both internally and externally, strategies for promoting the training are also proposed. Thus, the recommendations offered are aimed at health care organizations as a whole, rather than individual nursing leaders.

Recommendation 1

Develop and adopt a comprehensive workplace anti-bullying training program that includes a multidisciplinary forum. Hospital workplace anti-bullying training is essential but can only be effective if its content and format are suitable for the needs of the attendees. The first step in designing an effective workplace training program is thus ensuring full support of all involved and obtaining input regarding the content and delivery format. However, the goal should always be improving nursing culture and leadership development. At a minimum, curriculum should provide education on defining bullying, ensure that all attendees understand hospital involvement and expectations, provide explicit steps nurses should follow to report bullying incidents and conclude with a discussion of anti-bullying policies in place and the manner in which they are enforced and used to combat or penalize bullying behaviors.

Recommendation 2

In recognition of the importance of legislation in promoting desired behavior and mitigating unwanted workplace practices, a recommendation is that nursing leaders act as advocates against workplace bullying. Leaders serve as role models for their subordinates in their day-to-day interactions and should thus also assume an active role as frontline representatives that model moral principles for all employees. In addition to exhibiting the behaviors they wish their subordinates to emulate, nursing leaders should also emphasize legislative consequences of bullying and other forms of unacceptable workplace behavior.

The main goal of the health care profession, and nursing in particular, is to care for patients and promote wellbeing— something that can only be achieved in a healthy work environment that is safe and supportive.[30] Goals should also align with the human resources staff, because HR individuals can provide continual guidance on the legal ramifications for any violation of organizational policies. By ensuring that policies are in place and aligned with applicable legislation, organizations can create a framework for education and training that aims to ensure that each individual adheres to the ethical codes of practice, thus increasing efficiency in patient care as well as patient safety.

Recommendation 3

Based on the findings yielded by an extensive review of pertinent literature and the information provided by the research participants, a number of suggestions for improving anti-bullying measures in health care organizations can be offered. Having identified the key obstacles to the effective implementation of workplace anti-bullying training, as a part of this study, I developed a training method called **FIRE** (Fear, Intimidation, Retaliation, Everyone).

The FIRE approach goal is not only to mitigate the issues identified in extant studies and noted by the study participants, but also highlight the importance of addressing bullying in the nursing profession in a timely and effective manner. Implementation of FIRE within health care organizations could allow nurse leaders and their staff to learn to identify bullying. Leaders can also gain an understanding of underlying reasons behind failure of many bullying victims to report harmful acts.

In addition, the training could explore the common complaints from the bully, witness and victim perspectives. FIRE is a robust educational tool that I developed as a part of this investigation in order to stop further bullying acts and create a positive work environment.

In the FIRE acronym, the letter *F* stands for fear. Fear may be the initial predictor of bullying behaviors, because those afraid to speak out or report bullies are the most likely targets. Yet, because fear is subjective, it is very challenging to identify and address by leaders. Hence, as a part of any training initiative, leadership must be taught how to recognize subtle signs of fear, as well as appropriately deal with each individual case.

Broadly speaking, fear is a universal response to past or present traumatic events but can also occur when an individual is presented with an unfamiliar situation. Since causes of fear are so diverse, the emotional responses are also numerous. Nonetheless, in most cases, fear compromises an individual's emotional wellbeing, thus affecting work productivity and interaction with others.

In the workplace, specifically in the nursing profession, fear can be induced by both real and imagined threats. In many cases, fears of imagined situations can be more damaging, as confronting or avoiding such threats is not possible. Nurses affected by such issues perceive being victimized by the bully as likely and thus may have a stronger fearful response.

Fearful response often manifests as nurses complaining of being powerless and vulnerable. Nurses can be exposed to real threats, in which case fear often stems from being bullied in the past. As a means of coping with their fear of being subjected to workplace bullying, nurses may refuse interaction with the perpetrator, and are likely to complain bitterly about the job conditions. Nurses' dissatisfaction usually leads to increased absences, adversely affecting nursing practice. Therefore, nursing leadership must be mindful of these common sources of fear and look for any warning signs, especially anxiety, increased absenteeism and poor workplace relationships.

The second letter in the FIRE model, *I*, stands for intimidation. Unlike fear, intimidation is exhibited by the bully, who commits the harmful acts in order to induce the desired emotional responses from the victims. In the nursing profession, intimidation may be used as power influence among nurses to undermine individual confidence and self-esteem.

The nursing profession is highly stressful and some individuals cope with the complexity and high level of responsibility associated with their duties by seeking power and control in the workplace. Individuals may resort to intimidation of others as a means of increasing their sense of importance. When intimidation is prevalent in the workplace, bullying may pose a threat to the professional status of all members of the unit and should thus be a major concern for nursing leadership.

The need for intimidation indicates that an individual lacks the ability to communicate with others in a professional manner and uses bullying as a shield to mask personal deficiencies. Some nurses may even treat intimidation as a problem-solving tool because their unprofessionalism and poor social skills prevent them from dealing with issues in a more productive manner. This is typically manifested through refusal to cooperate, impatience to answer questions and unwillingness to support team goals, ultimately compromising patient safety. Intimidation should thus be the focus of strategies aimed at improving workplace standards, as it undermines performance and attitudes of all team members.

R, as the third letter in the FIRE acronym, stands for retaliation. Retaliation often serves as a self-defense mechanism in bullying encounters. However, for nurse leaders, retaliatory behaviors should be the sign of dysfunctional relationships among employees. When the intentional cruelty associated with bullying is reciprocated in equal measure by the victim, the harmful behaviors perpetuate. Since retaliation occurs instead of communication, the bullying behaviors are never resolved. Hence, leadership must place emphasis on protecting the victim from the bully and offering other channels for dealing with workplace bullying, thus preventing retaliation.

Although not all nurses have the same capacity for dealing with stress, nursing leaders should strive to identify staff at the greatest risk and offer individuals whose rights have been violated protection and reassurance. Retaliation can take both organizational and individual form. Organizational retaliation occurs when management takes a negative stance against an employee who may be demoted, denied a pay raise or promotion, given a poor employee evaluation, denied transfer to another department or even fired. Individual retaliation is usually peer-directed and manifests as unjust treatment. Some examples include:

- Antisocial behaviors (lack of interpersonal interaction with peers or rude behaviors);
- Work overload or unfair work assignments;
- Silence from peers (refusal to answer questions or denying help or resources);
- Peer jealousy; and

- Identity threat (diminished sense of self-worth and competency).

The *E* in the FIRE model stands for everyone, because everyone has the potential to be both the victim and the bully. Situations may arise in which intimidating behavior occurs that may impede the ability to respond to a threatening individual or event appropriately.

Leadership must be sufficiently trained to recognize situations that may result in bullying and address the underlying issues in a timely manner, before they escalate further. Nurse leaders have a responsibility to recognize and manage workplace bullying to protect all employees through policies and practical support. Absence of effective leadership and appropriate policy measures may result in compromising victims' ethical and moral values.

A display of concern and personal warmth towards everyone, a positive example for all employees to follow, creating the necessary impetus for more permanent changes in the workforce. Training programs, such as FIRE, should be offered to allow all staff members to gain necessary information and skills to not only respond to bullying effectively, but also assist victims when needed.

FIRE is unique in its approach to the bullying issue and this acronym both implies and emphasizes the urgency with which this problem must be addressed. Because of the prevalence of workplace bullying, each step in the program represents a different level, denoted by the FIRE acronym. Nurse leaders may use this groundbreaking method to quickly identify bullying occurrences and effectively change the way nurses perceive and react to bullying within their units.

ॐ

Recommendation 4

The scope of workplace anti-bullying training could expand to include the entire nursing profession and community. For bullying to be eradicated from health care institutions, training must be comprehensive and become part of the curriculum taught to nursing students. In addition, continuous workplace initiatives should be in place, so that newly qualified nurses as well as veterans can augment their knowledge and skills on a regular basis.

The nurses who took part in the present study frequently noted lack of communication in their individual interviews. This issue can be easily mitigated by scheduling a daily focus group session in all nursing units. Having a platform for raising concerns, including bullying, would encourage victims and witnesses to report bullying acts in a timely manner. Having a platform for discussing concerns might decrease bullying occurrences in individual units because the open dialogue on bullying actions could expose the perpetrators, making them less likely to continue committing harmful acts.

Nursing leadership should lead the focus group sessions. Presence of superiors in these daily meetings could not only signal their support for anti-bullying measures but could also allow them to react to any issues in a timely and effective manner. Fardellone and Click[186] suggested that nurses are more likely to mimic actions or behaviors exhibited by a mentor, a charge nurse or a member of the nursing leadership team. Through group discussions, nurses might gain a better understanding of the problems others are facing, ask questions and offer solutions to issues that arise within their units.

In addition, focus group discussions could promote social interactions as well as the use of group behavioral contracts. Group discussions could pave the way for creating an atmosphere in which all team members are aware of actions that are acceptable and those that are not, and are thus subject to disciplinary measures. Human resources should also play a proactive role in promoting organizational guidelines and serve as a supportive resource for nurses affected by bullying.

∞

RESEARCHER REFLECTIONS

This study was motivated by my realization, as a nursing director, that health care organizations, hospitals in particular, are insufficiently proactive in eradicating bullying from the workplace. The lack of proactivity translates to inadequate attention given to workplace anti-bullying training, allowing such harmful acts to perpetuate, potentially endangering or harming the patients. Bullying behaviors in nursing have been extensively studied, with many recommendations offered for nursing education and nursing practice.

However, incongruence between these research-based guidelines and practical implementation evidently exists, suggesting that nursing leadership is rather content with respect to addressing bullying behaviors in the workplace. Even though bullying is present in hospitals, given the absence of state and federal laws that prohibit bullying among co-workers, some health care workers see it as a necessary part of their job.

Bullying, in any form and in any setting, is never acceptable and more concerted efforts must be made to ensure that nurses feel safe in the workplace. The nurses who were interviewed as a part of the present study expressed their dissatisfaction with the lax attitude toward bullying in their units. Thirteen explicitly stated that no personal or legal protective mechanisms are available to nurses who are victims of bullying. As a result, those who have experienced or witnessed such harmful behavior felt they had to resort to their personal coping strategies to deal with these bullying experiences.

Analyses of nurses' feedback also revealed that three knew the precise definition of bullying, whereas the other nurses in the study did not. The lack of clarity about the definition of bullying for the remaining 11 nurses could also contribute to the pervasiveness of bullying in the workplace, as both victims and witnesses may feel uncertain whether some offensive behaviors or verbal altercations could be classified as bullying.

In addition, the lack of clarity in the definition also made it difficult for several participants to determine whether they had received anti-bullying training, or if any was offered in their organization. Extant research confirms that hospitals often offer workplace anti-bullying training as part of more comprehensive professional development initiatives, or education on codes of conduct, which contributes to the confusion. This ambiguity is aptly summarized by participant RN14, who said, "I think that what you have taken on is a specific topic, but I think it's equal to everything else."

RN08's comment that "they have to have that consequence" is also highly indicative of the type and format of training nurses expect. In sum, for workplace anti-bullying training to have practical effects, it must be provided to all employees; attendance must be mandatory and should be monitored, and the outcomes must be measured through appropriate tools. In addition, enforcement of disciplinary actions should be emphasized, as this would serve as a deterrent for perpetrators. Adopting this approach is likely to result in a positive shift in the work environment for nurses.

During the telephone interviews, all participants expressed their frustrations with the quality of the training they had been offered to date. They used very strong words, such as "Kind of a joke," "It's not very effective training," "It doesn't require a lot of effort on our part" and "It's meaningless." Comments such as these were disheartening, though the nurses' openness during the interviews was encouraging, as the openness meant that all participants felt comfortable sharing their views candidly. In fact, most of the interviewees appeared to be glad that someone is addressing the anti-bullying training and expressed that this gives them hope for the future of nursing profession.

As a nursing director, I have attained immense benefits conducting this research, as I now have a much deeper understanding of leadership challenges and obstacles to realization of any initiatives in hospitals. Although this study was limited in scope by the small sample, the insights gained still have the potential to influence nursing leadership, prompting them to develop effective educational training programs.

Because the goal of the nursing profession is to deliver quality care to all patients, noble health care professionals must be given the support they need to do their jobs safely and effectively without fear. Professionals can benefit from more collegial relationships and supportive leadership. For me as a nursing leader, the main benefit of completing this study has resulted in a greater resolve and dedication to explore colleagues' life experiences on a sensitive topic. This study has brought about a change in my personal viewpoint on health care.

⚜

Limitations

As with any study of this nature, this research was affected by several limitations. First, all participants were nurses employed in a hospital, therefore, their comments may not be representative of views held by nurses working in different health care settings (e.g., clinics) and at different organizational positions (e.g., management). In addition, data collection was performed via individual telephone interviews, preventing observation of the interviewee's body language, and other cues that are readily apparent in face-to-face interviews.

Moreover, interviews were guided by a predefined set of questions, whereby the potential to broaden the scope of discussion was limited. Thus, including a greater number of participants, from more diverse settings, and allowing them to speak about other issues pertaining to workplace bullying might have increased the credibility, dependability, transferability and confirmability of the study. Supplementing individual interviews with focus group discussions and questionnaire surveys involving a greater number of respondents may have facilitated triangulation of study findings. The limitations presented should be considered when planning research studies of this type.

Recommendations for Future Research

Research efforts regarding nurses and workplace bullying are of interest to nurses, nursing management, hospital administration and state and federal officials. A recommendation is to replicate this study with nursing students as research participants. The results of this dissertation study indicate that it may be valuable to seek nurses' views on other forms of education, such as leadership training. Future studies in this field could also seek to identify the major barriers to hospitals implementing effective workplace anti-bullying training programs. Given limited research on workplace anti-bullying training, especially studies related to hospital settings as expressed by Livington et al.,[125] further research is needed to understand bullying in the hospital workplace.

Future research studies should explore how the Unity of Command principle supports workplace anti-bullying training in the hospital setting. Unity of Command ensures that hospitals are stable and orderly environments that are fully protective and supportive of all staff members, with the ultimate goal of providing the best service to the patients.

Under the Unity of Command structure, nursing leadership can implement one plan (i.e., workplace anti-bullying training) for all employees whose roles lean toward similar objectives. The Unity of Command principle helps leaders select the appropriate person using a systematic and structured approach, which is also applied to assign a specific activity to each of the nurses, as well as for acquisition and distribution of material resources.

Future research should focus on workplace anti-bullying training programs and the experiences of attendees in other nursing departments and occupations within the organization. Research aiming to survey a different subset of nurses or student nurses, or to implement Unity of Command principles, could also be conducted in other types of organizations, such as educational nursing institutions, where nursing educators' and students' experiences of workplace anti-bullying training could be examined.

CHAPTER FIVE SUMMARY

In this chapter, the themes yielded by the thematic analysis of individual telephone interviews held with 14 acute care nurses in the Oklahoma City metropolitan area were analyzed and interpreted in the context of the findings reported in the pertinent literature. The chapter commences with an interpretation of each theme, accompanied by direct quotes exemplifying the participants' viewpoints. Six themes emerged from the data analysis and have particular relevance for future anti-bullying training initiatives.

The workplace anti-bullying training that most nurses receive is ineffective. Thus, the main objective of this research project was to ascertain whether the training the participating nurses received had an effect upon their job performance and patient safety. In addition to examining coping strategies these nurses adopted due to the anti-bullying training received, they were prompted to offer suggestions for improvements.

They all concurred that lack of effective workplace anti-bullying training degraded staff morale, potentially endangering the patients, while allowing bullies to continue exhibiting unprofessional behaviors.

Chapter Five Notes

_____
_____
_____
_____
_____
_____
_____
_____
_____
_____
_____
_____
_____
_____
_____
_____
_____
_____
_____
_____
_____
_____
_____
_____
_____
_____
_____
_____
_____
_____

CONCLUSION

The qualitative study reported in this thesis aimed to gain in-depth insights regarding acute care nurses' experiences of workplace anti-bullying training and the perceived impact this initiative had on their ability to perform their job duties. Participants shared their views in individual telephone interviews and their responses were subsequently analyzed to reveal common themes.

The findings yielded indicate that the nurses considered the training their organizations offered to the nursing staff was ineffective in resolving workplace bullying issues. The participants relied on self-developed strategies to deal with workplace bullying, citing awareness and self-control techniques, such as personal internal values or previous experiences in their workplace practice, as the most effective. The gap between professional development training and practical implementation of information and knowledge gained is evident, calling for a revision of current training practices. Making the training offered more relevant to the attendees can strengthen nurses and nursing leaders in incorporating consistent training for recognizing workplace bullying issues effectively.

When redesigning the training curricula and modes of delivery, decision makers should consider the four primary shortcomings of workplace anti-bullying training in a hospital setting identified by the nurses who took part in the present study. However, it is essential to note that the effectiveness of any program is largely dependent on the support received by all stakeholders, particularly management. Thus, in addition to providing the appropriate content and training methods, any broader hospital issues that could jeopardize successful program implementation must be addressed.

The complex issues never have an easy solution, however, the participants did share some creative ideas for improving workplace training, such as utilizing innovative means of communication, greater leadership involvement and internal policy support that may address bullying acts or improve workplace anti-bullying training.

Health care organizations across the United States aim to incorporate training for all future and existing professionals and bullying prevention strategies should be given high priority in this endeavor.

REFERENCES

1. Oyeleye, O., Hanson, P., O'Connor, N., & Dunn, D. (2013). Relationship of workplace incivility, stress, and burnout on nurses' turnover intentions and psychological empowerment. *The Journal of Nursing Administration*, 43, 536–542. doi:10.1097/nna.0b013e3182a3e8c9

2. Alberts, H. C., Hazen, H. D., & Theobald, R. B. (2010). Classroom incivilities: The challenge of interactions between college students and instructors in the U.S. *Journal of Geography in Higher Education*, 34, 439-462. doi:10.1080%2F03098260903502679

3. Broome, B. S., & Williams-Evans, S. (2011). Bullying in a caring profession: Reasons, results, and recommendations. *Journal of Psychosocial Nursing & Mental Health Services*, 49(10), 30-35. doi:10.3928/02793695-20110831-02

4. Anderson, K. (2011). Workplace aggression and violence: Nurses and midwives say no. *Australian Nursing Journal*, 19(1), 26–29.

5. Einarsen, S., Hoel, H., Zapf, D., & Cooper, C. L. (Eds.). (2011). *Bullying and Harassment in the Workplace: Developments in*

REFERENCES

Theory, Research and Practice (2nd ed.). Boca Raton, FL: Taylor & Francis.

6. Longo, J. (2010). Combating disruptive behaviors: Strategies to promote a healthy work environment. *The Online Journal of Issues in Nursing,* 15(1), Manuscript 5. doi:10.3912/OJIN.Vol15No01Man05

7. Etienne, E. (2014). Exploring workplace bullying in nursing. *Workplace Health & Safety,* 62, 6-11. doi:10.3928/21650799-20131220-02

8. Lieber, L. D. (2010). How workplace bullying affects the bottom line. *Employment Relations Today,* 37, 91-101. doi:10.1002/ert.20314 Lincoln, Y., & Guba, E. (2008). *Naturalistic validity, or trustworthiness, is the qualitative equivalent of validation approaches in inquiry.* Beverly Hills, CA: Sage.

9. Undheim, A. M., & Sund, A. M. (2011). Bullying -A hidden factor behind somatic symptoms? *Acta Paediatrica,* 100, 496-498. doi:10.1111/j.1651-2227.2011.02174x

10. Fry, B. J. (2010). *Fast Facts for the Clinical Nurse Manager: Managing a Changing Workplace in a Nutshell.* New York, NY: Springer.

11. Marty, M., Segal, D., & Coolidge, F. (2010). Relationships among dispositional coping strategies, suicidal ideation, and protective factors against suicide in older adults. *Aging & Mental Health,* 14, 1015-1023. doi:10.1080/13607863.2010.501068

12. Skehan, J. (2015). Nursing leaders: Strategies for eradicating bullying in the workforce. *Nurse Leaders,* 13(2), 60-62. doi:10.1016/j.mnl.2014.07.015

13. Thobaben, M. (2011). Bullying in the nursing profession. *Home Health Care Management & Practice,* 23, 477-479. doi:10.1177/1084822311413556

14. Idsoe, T., Dyregrov, A., & Idsoe, E. C. (2012). Bullying and PTSD symptoms. *Journal of Abnormal Child Psychology,* 40, 901-911. doi:10.1007/s10802-012-9620-0

15. Yoon, S., & Kim, J. H. (2013). Job-related stress, emotional labor, and depressive symptoms among Korean nurses. *Journal of Nursing Scholarship*, 45, 169-176. doi:10.1111/jnu.120

16. Conte, T. M. (2010). Pediatric oncology nurse and grief education: A telephone survey. *Journal of Pediatric Oncology Nursing*, 28, 93–99. doi:10.1177/1043454210377900

17. Hildebrandt, L. (2012). Providing grief resolution as an oncology nurse retention strategy. *Clinical Journal of Oncology Nursing*, 16, 601–606. doi:10.1188/12.cjon.601-606

18. Abrahamson, K., Anderson, J., Anderson, M., Suitor, J., & Pillemer, K. (2010). The cumulative influence of conflict on nursing home staff. *Research in Gerontological Nursing*, 3(1), 39-48. doi:10.3928/19404921-20090731-06

19. Frederick, D. (2014). Bullying, mentoring, and patient care. *Association of Operating Room Nurses Journal*, 99, 587-593. doi:10.1016/j.aorn.2013.10.023

20. Namie, G., & Namie, R. F. (2011). *The bully-free workplace: Stop jerks, weasels, and snakes from killing your organization.* Hoboken, NJ: Wiley.

21. Hutchinson, M., & Hurley, J. (2012). Exploring leadership capability and emotional intelligence as moderators of workplace bullying. *Journal of Nursing Management*, 21, 553-562. doi:10.1111/j.1365-2834.2012.01372.x

22. Rhodes, C., Pullen, A., Vickers, M. H., Clegg, S. R., & Pitsis, A. (2010). Violence and workplace bullying: What are an organization's ethical responsibilities? *Administrative Theory & Praxis*, 32(1), 96-115. Retrieved from http://www.mesharpe.com/mall/results1.asp?acr=atp

23. Sloan, L. D., Matyok, T., Schmitz, C. L., & Short, G. F. L. (2010). A story to tell: Bullying and mobbing in the workplace. *International Journal of Business and Social Science*, 1(3), 87-91. Retrieved from http://www.ijbssnet.com/

24. Taylor, C., & Zeng, H. (2011). Case study in threats of workplace violence from a non-supervisory basis. *Mustang Journal of Law and Legal Studies*, 2, 55-64. doi:10.1016/j.avb.2012.08.004

25. Kinnaman, J. E. S., & Bellack, A. S. (2012). *Social Skills. Core Principles for Practice* [Online]. doi:10.1002/9781118470886.ch10

26. Alexander, L. L. (2012). Burnout: Impact on nursing. *NetCE Continuing Education.* Retrieved from http://www.netce.com/827/course_3143.pdf

26a. Gaffney, D., DeMarco, R., Hofmeyer, A., Vessey, J., & Budin, W. C. (2012). Making things right: nurses' experiences with workplace bullying—A grounded theory. *Nursing Research and Practice, 2012,* 1-10. doi:10.1155/2012/243210

27. Blum, H., & Beck, D. (2015). Shared responsibility approach: How to resolve bullying in three steps. *InterAction - The Journal of Solution Focus in Organisations, 7*(2), 88-96. Retrieved from http://www.ingentaconnect

28. Kramer, M., Maguire, P., & Brewer, B. B. (2011). Clinical nurses in magnet hospitals confirm productive, healthy unit work environments. *Journal of Nursing Management,* 19, 5–17. doi:10.1111/j.1365-2834.2010.01211.x

29. Schein, E. (2010). *Organizational Culture and Leadership* (4th ed.). San Francisco, CA: Jossey-Bass.

30. Papa, A., Venella, J., (2013). Workplace violence in healthcare: Strategies for advocacy. OJIN: *The Online Journal of Issues in Nursing,* 18(1). doi:10.3912/OJIN.Vol18No01Man05

31. Knudson, L. (2014). Developing internal talent necessary to fill perioperative leadership roles. *AORN Journal,* 99(2), C1-C9. doi:10.1016/S0001-2092(13)01401-4

32. Kemparaj, U., & Chavan, S. (2013). Qualitative research: A brief description. *Indian Journal of Medical Sciences,* 67, 89-98. doi:10.4103/0019-5359.121127

33. Jones, A., & Steen, M. (2013). Safeguarding and qualitative research. *Nurse Education Today,* 33, 1095. doi:10.1016/j.nedt.2012.12.005 151. Joint Commission Accreditation of Healthcare Organization. (2008). *Behaviors That Undermine a Culture of Safety.* Retrieved from https://www.jointcommission.org/assets/1/18/SEA_40.PDF

34. Peter, S. (2010). Qualitative research methods in mental health. *Evidence-Based Mental Health*, 13, 35-40. doi:10.1136/ebmh.13.2.35

35. Campbell, S. (2014). What is qualitative research? *Clinical Laboratory Science*, 27(1), 3. Retrieved from http://www.clin-lab-publications.com

36. Nielsen, D. S. (2011). Overview of qualitative research methods. *Bone*, 48, S51. doi:10.1016/j.bone.2011.03.008

37. Leedy, P. D., & Ormrod, J. E. (2010). *Practical Research: Planning and Design* (9th ed.), p 62. Upper Saddle River, NJ: Pearson.

38. Berg, B. (2009). *Qualitative Research Methods for the Social Science* (7th ed.). Boston, MA: Allyn & Bacon.

39. Merriam, S. B. (2009). *Qualitative Research: A Guide to Design and Implementation.* San Francisco, CA: Wiley.

40. Wolf, L. A., Carmen, M. J., Henderson, D., Kamienski, M., Koziol-McLain, J., Manton, A., & Moon, M. D. (2013). Evaluating evidence for practice. *Journal of Emergency Nursing*, 39, 197-199. doi:10.1016/j.jen.2012.11.009

41. Coupland, R. (2013). The role of health-related data in promoting the security of health care in armed conflict and other emergencies. *International Review Red Cross*, 95(889), 61–71. doi:10.1017/s1816383113000647

42. Stagg, S. J., & Sheridan, D. J. (2010). Effectiveness of bullying and violence prevention program: A systematic review. *American Association of Occupational Health Nurses Journal*, 58, 419-424. doi:10.3928/08910162-20100916-02

43. Needham, I., McKenna, K., Kingma, M., & Oud, N. (2012). *Violence in the health sector. Third International Conference on Violence in the Health Sector Linking Local Initiative With Global Learning.* Vancouver, Canada. Retrieved from http://www.oudconsultancy.nl/Resources/Proceedings_3rd_Work place_Violence_2012.pdf

44. Laszlo, A., & Krippner, S. (1998). Systems theories: Their origins, foundations, and development. *Advances in Psychology*, pp. 8, 47–74. doi:10.1016/s0166-4115(98)80017-4

45. Viollis, P. (2005). *Most workplace violence avoidable.* Retrieved from http://www.businessinsurance.com/von Bertalanffy, L. (1968). *General Systems Theory: Essays on its Foundation and Development.* (p. 1) New York, NY: George Braziller.

46. Berry, P., Gillespie, G., Gates, D., & Schafer, J. (2012). Novice nurse productivity following workplace bullying. *Journal of Nursing Scholarship*, 44, 80-87. doi:10.1111/J.1547-5069.2011.01436.x

47. Fujishiro, K., Gee, G. C., & De Castro, A. B. (2011). Associations of workplace aggression with work-related well-being among nurses in the Philippines. *American Journal of Public Health*, 101, 861-867. doi:10.2105/ajph.2009.188144

48. Spector, P. E., Zhou, Z. E., & Che, X. X. (2014). Nurse exposure to physical and nonphysical violence, bullying, and sexual harassment: A quantitative review. *International Journal of Nursing Studies*, 51, 72-84. doi:10.1016/j.ijnurstu.2013.01.010

49. Laschinger, H. K. (2014). Impact of workplace mistreatment on patient safety risk and nurse-assessed patient outcomes. *The Journal of Nursing Administration*, 44, 284–290. doi:10.1097/nna.0000000000000068

50. Van Manen, M. (2007). Phenomenology of practice. *Phenomenology & Practice*, 1. Retrieved from http://www.maxvanmanen.com/files/2011/04/2007-Phenomenology-of-Practice.pdf

51. DeVeaux, R. D., Velleman, P. D., & Bock, D. E. (2009). *Intro Stats* (3rd ed.). Boston, MA : Pearson Addison Wesley.

52. Langdride, D. (2007). *Phenomenological Psychology: Theory, Research and Method.* Upper Saddle River, NJ: Pearson Education.

53. Moustakas, C. (1994). *Phenomenological Research Methods.* Thousand Oaks, CA: Sage.

REFERENCES

54. Simon, M. K., & Goes, J. (2013). *Dissertation and Scholarly Research: Recipes for Success.* Seattle, WA: Dissertation Success.

55. Moye, M. (2010). *Nursing Hostility: What causes horizontal violence between nurses and what steps can individuals take to bring it to an end.* Retrieved from http://nursing.advanceweb.com/editorial/content/editorial.aspx?cc=214570

56. Hickson, J. (2013). New nurses' perceptions of hostility and job satisfaction. JONA: *The Journal of Nursing Administration, 43,* 293–301. doi:10.1097/nna.0b013e31828eebc9

57. Vie, T., Glaso, L., & Einarsen, S. (2011). Health outcomes and self-labeling as a victim of workplace bullying. *Journal of Psychosomatic Research,* 70, 37-43. doi:10.1016/j.jpsychores.2010.06.007

58. Leymann, H. (1990). Mobbing and psychological terror at workplaces. *Violence and Victims,* 5(2), 119-126. Retrieved from http://www.mobbingportal.com/LeymannV%26V1990(3).pdf

59. Niedl, K. (1996). Mobbing and Well-being: Economic and Personnel Development Implications. *European Journal of Work and Organizational Psychology,* 5(2), 239–249. doi:10.1080/13594329608414857

60. Vartia, M. (1996). The sources of bullying: Psychological work environment and organizational climate. *European Journal of Work & Organizational Psychology,* 5(2), 203-296. doi: 10.1080/13594329608414855

61. MacIntosh, J. (2005). Experiences of workplace bullying in a rural area. *Issues in Mental Health Nursing,* 26, 893-910. doi:10.1080/01612840500248189

62. MacIntosh, J., Wuest, J., Gray, M. M., & Cronkhite, M. (2010). Workplace bullying in health care affects the meaning of work. *Qualitative Health Research,* 20,1128-1141. doi:10.1177/1049732310369804

63. Koo, H. (2007). A time line of the evolution of school bullying in differing social contexts. *Asia Pacific Education Review*, 8(1), 107–116. doi:10.1007/bf03025837

64. Yamada, D. C. (2004). Crafting a legislative response to workplace bullying. *Employee Rights and Employment Policy Journal*, 8, 475. Retrieved from http://papers.ssrn.com/sol3/cf_dev/AbsByAuth.cfm?per_id=3037 25-4

65. Yamada, D. C. (2010). *Workplace Bullying and American Employment Law: A 10 Year Progress Report and Assessment.* Retrieved from http://www.jil.go.jp/english/reports/documents/jilpt-reports/no.12_u.s.a..pdf

66. Davidson, D., & Harrington, K. (2012). Workplace bullying: It's not just about lunch money anymore. *Southern Journal of Business and Ethics*, 4, 93-99. Retrieved from https:// http://www.salsb.org/sjbe

67. Kaplan, J. F. (2010). Help is on the way: A recent case shed light on workplace bullying. *Houston Law Review*, 47(1), 141-173.

68. Martin, W., & LaVan, H. (2010). Workplace bullying: A review of litigated cases. *Employee Responsibilities and Rights Journal*, 22(3), 175–194. doi:10.1007/s10672-009-9140-4

69. Bowen, B., Privitera, M. R., & Bowie, V. (2011). Reducing workplace violence by creating healthy workplace environments. *Journal of Aggression, Conflict and Peace Research*, 3, 185-198. doi:10.1108/17596591111187710

70. Workplace Bullying Institute. (2010). *Results of the 2010 WBI U.S. Workplace Survey.* Retrieved from http://www.workplacebullying.org/docs/WBIsurvey2010.pdf

71. Simons, S. R., & Mawn, B. (2010). Bullying in the workplace-A qualitative study of newly licensed registered nurses. *American Association of Occupational Health Nurses Journal*, 58, 305–311. doi:10.3928/08910162-20100616-02

72. Veechio, N., Scuffham, P. A., Hilton, M. F., & Whiteford, H. A. (2011). Work-related injury in the nursing profession: an

investigation of modifiable factors. *Journal of Advanced Nursing*, 67, 1067-1078. doi:10.1111/j.1365-2648.2010.05544.x

73. Ali, W. (2012). Bullying. *Nevada RNformation*, 21(1), 16. Retrieved from http://www.nursingald.com/articles/4105-bullying?query=bullying&s=84

74. Baker, C. (2012). Nurses eating their young: Are we teaching students more than nursing skills? *Oklahoma Nurse*, 57(1), 9. Retrieved from http://www.oknurses.com

75. Indvik, J., & Johnson, P. R. (2012.). Lawsuits walk in on two feet: The bully in the workplace. *Journal of Organizational Culture* 16(2), 73-77.

76. Brancato, V. C. (2007). Psychological empowerment and use of empowering teaching behaviors among baccalaureate nursing faculty. *Journal of Nursing Education*, 46, 537–544.

77. Fletcher, K. (2006). Beyond dualism: Leading out of oppression. *Nursing Forum*, 41(2), 50–59. doi:10.1111/j.1744-6198.2006.00039.x

78. Farrell, G. A., & Shafiei, T. (2012). Workplace aggression, including bullying in nursing and midwifery: A descriptive survey (the SWAB study). *International Journal of Nursing Studies*, 49, 1423-1431. doi:10.1016/j.ijnurstu.2012.06.007

79. Ariza-Montes, A., Muniz, N. M., Montero-Simó, M. J., & Araque-Padilla, R. (2013). Workplace bullying among healthcare workers. *International Journal of Environmental Research and Public Health*, 10, 3121-3139. doi:10.3390/ijerph10083121

80. Samnani, A., & Singh, P. (2012). 20 years of workplace bullying research: A review of the antecedents and consequences of bullying in the workplace. *Aggression and Violent Behavior*, 17, 581-589. doi:10.1016/j.avb.2012.08.004

81. Power, J. L., Brotheridge, C. M., Blenkinsopp, J., Bowes-Sperry, L., Bozionelos, N., Buzády, Z., Nnedumm, A. U. O. (2013). Acceptability of workplace bullying: A comparative study on six contents. *Journal of Business Research*, 66, 374-380. doi:10.1016/j.jbusres.2011.08.018

82. Center, D. L. (2011). Mandates for patient safety: Are they enough to create a culture of civility in health care? *The Journal of Continuing Education in Nursing*, 42,16-17. doi:10.3928/00220124-20110105-04

83. Dzurec, L., & Bromley, G. (2012). Speaking of workplace bullying. *Journal of Professional Nursing*, 28, 247-254. doi:10.1016/j.profnurs.2012.01.004

84. Vickers, M. H. (2010). Introduction-bullying, mobbing, and violence in public service workplaces: The shifting sands of "acceptable" violence. *Administrative Theory & Praxis*, 32, 7-24. doi:10.2753/atp1084-1806320101

85. American Psychiatric Association (2014). *Posttraumatic stress disorder fact sheet*. Arlington, VA: Author.

86. National Center for PTSD. (2013). *Understanding PTSD*. Retrieved from http://www.ptsd.va.gov

87. Creamer, M., Wade, D., Fletcher, S., & Forbes, D. (2011). PTSD among military personnel. *International Review of Psychiatry*, 23, 160-165. doi:10.3109/09540261.2011.559456

88. Lancaster, S. L., Melka, S. E., & Rodriguez, B. F. (2011). Emotional predictors of PTSD symptoms. *Psychological Trauma: Theory, Research, Practice and Policy*, 3, 313-317. doi:10.1037/a0022751

89. Lavoie, S., Talbot, L. R., & Mathieu, L. (2011). Post-traumatic stress disorder symptoms among emergency nurses: Their perspective and a "tailor-made" solution. *Journal of Advanced Nursing*, 67, 1514-1522. doi:10.1111/j.1365-2648.2010.05584

90. Sabella, D. (2012). PTSD among our returning veterans. *American Journal of Nursing*, 112(11), 48-52. doi:10.1097/01.NAJ.0000422255.95706.40

91. National Institute of Mental Health. (2013). Post-Traumatic Stress Disorder. Retrieved from http://www.nimh.nih.gov/health/publications/post-traumatic-stress-disorder-easy-to-read/index.shtm

92. Beck, C. (2011). Secondary traumatic stress in nurses: A systematic review. *Archives of Psychiatric Nursing*, 25, 1-10. doi:10.1016/j.apnu.2010.05.005

93. Lanctôt, N., & Guay, S. (2014). The aftermath of workplace violence among healthcare workers: A systematic literature review of the consequences. *Aggression and Violent Behavior*, 19(5), 492–501. doi:10.1016/j.avb.2014.07.010

94. Gillespie, G. L., Bresler, S., Gates, D. M., & Succop, P. (2013). Posttraumatic stress symptomatology among emergency department workers following workplace aggression. *Workplace Health Safety*, 61(6), 247–254. doi:10.3928/21650799-20130516-07

95. deBoer, J., Lok, A., Van't Verlaat, E., Duivenvoorden, H. J., Bakker, A. B., & Smit, B. J. (2011). Work-related critical incidents in hospital-based health care providers and the risk of post-traumatic stress symptoms, anxiety, and depression: A meta-analysis. *Social Science & Medicine*, 73, 316–326. doi:10.1016/j.socscimed.2011.05.009

96. Skogstad, M., Skorstad, M., Lie, A., Conradi, H. S., Heir, T., & Weisaeth, L. (2013). Work-related post-traumatic stress disorder. *Occupational Medicine*, 63, 175-182. doi:10.1093/occmed/kqt003

97. Mealer, M., Jones, J., & Moss, M. (2012). A qualitative study of resilience and posttraumatic stress disorder in United States ICU nurses. *Intensive Care Medicine*, 38, 1445-1451. doi:10.1007/s00134-012-2600-6

98. Mealer, M., Jones, J., Newman, J., McFann, K. K., Rothbaum, B., & Moss, M. (2012). The presence of resilience is associated with a healthier psychological profile in intensive care unit (ICU) nurses: Results of a national survey. *International Journal of Nursing Studies*, 49(3), 292–299. doi:10.1016/j.ijnurstu.2011.09.015

99. Czaja, A., Moss, M., & Mealer, M. (2012). Symptoms of posttraumatic stress among pediatric acute care nurses. *Journal of Pediatric Nursing*, 27, 357-365 doi:10.1016/j.pedn.2011.04.024

100. Opie, T., Dollard, M., Wakerman, J., MacLeod, M., Knight, S., Dunn, R. (2010). Trends in the workplace violence in the remote area nursing workforce. *Australian Journal of Advanced Nursing*, 27(4). 13-23. Retrieved from http://www.ajan.com.au/Vol27/27- 4_Opie.pdf

101. Rodwell, J. J., & Demir, D. D. (2012). Psychological consequences of bullying for hospital and aged care nurses. *International Nursing Review*, 59, 539-546.

102. Woodrow, C., & Guest, D. E. (2012). Public violence, staff harassment and the wellbeing of nursing staff: An analysis of national survey data. *Health Services Management Research*, 25(1), 24–30. doi:10.1258/hsmr.2011.011019

103. Letvak, S., Ruhm, C. J., & McCoy, T. (2012). Depression in hospital-employed nurses. *Clinical Nurse Specialist*, 26, 177–182. doi:10.1097/nur.0b013e3182503ef0

104. Cavanaugh, C., Campbell, J., & Messing, J. T. (2014). A longitudinal study of the impact of cumulative violence victimization on comorbid posttraumatic stress and depression among female nurses and nursing personnel. *Workplace Health Safety*, 62(6), 224–232. doi:10.3928/21650799-20140514-01

105. Rodríguez-Muñoz, A., Moreno-Jiménez, B., Sanz Vergel, A. I., & Garrosa Hernández, E. (2010). Post-traumatic symptoms among victims of workplace bullying: Exploring gender differences and shattered assumptions. *Journal of Applied Social Psychology*, 40, 2616-2635. doi:10.1111/j.1559-1816.2010.00673.x

106. Rogers, B. (2011). Nursing occupational injury and stress. In *Encyclopedia of Nursing Research*. Retrieved from http://search.credoreference.com/content/entry/ spennurres/nursing_occupational_injury_and_stress/0

107. Epstein, D. G. (2010). Extinguish workplace stress. *Nursing Management*, 41(10), 34–37. doi:10.1097/01.numa.0000388295.31857.a2

108. Cleary, M., Hunt, G. E., Walter, G., & Robertson, M. (2009). Dealing with bullying in the workplace: Toward zero tolerance. *Journal of Psychosocial Nursing & Mental Health Services*, 47(12), 34-41. doi:10.3928/02793695-20091103-03

109. Cleary, M., Hunt, G., & Horsfall, J. (2010). Identifying and addressing bullying in nursing. *Issues in Mental Health Nursing*, 31, 331-335. doi:10.3109/01612840903308531

110. Toh, S. G., Ang, E., & Devi, M. K. (2012). Systematic review on the relationship between the nursing shortage and job satisfaction, stress and burnout levels among nurses in oncology/hematology settings. *International Journal of Evidence-Based Healthcare*, 10, 126–141. doi:10.1111/j.1744-1609.2012.00271.x

111. Hecktman, H. M. (2012). Stress in pediatric oncology nurses. *Journal of Pediatric Oncology Nursing*, 29, 356–361. doi:10.1177/1043454212458367

112. Bush, N. J. (2009). Compassion fatigue: Are you at risk? *Oncology Nursing Forum*, 36, 24–28. doi:10.1188/09.onf.24-28

113. Birks, M., Budden, L. M., Stewart, L., & Chapman, Y. (2014). Turning the tables: The growth of upward bullying in nursing academia. *Journal of Advanced Nursing*, 70, 1685–1687. doi:10.1111/jan.12317

114. Alacacioglu, A., Yavuzsen, T., Dirioz, M., Oztop, I., & Yilmaz, U. (2009). Burnout in nurses and physicians working at an oncology department. *Psycho-Oncology*, 18, 543–548. doi:10.1002/pon.1432

115. Medland, J., Howard-Ruben, J., & Whitaker, E. (2004). Fostering psychosocial wellness in oncology nurses: Addressing burnout and social support in the workplace. *Oncology Nursing Forum*, 31(1), 47-54.

116. King-Jones, M. (2011). Horizontal violence and the socialization of new nurses. *Creative Nursing*, 17, 80-86. doi:10.1891/1078-4535.17.2.80

117. Roberts, S. J., Scherer, L. L., & Bowyer, C. J. (2011). Job stress and incivility: What role does psychological capital play?

REFERENCES

Journal of Leadership & Organizational Studies, 18(4), 449-458. doi:10.1177/1548051811409044

118. Roberts, R. K., & Grubb, P. L. (2013). The consequences of nursing stress and need for integrated solutions. *Rehabilitative Nursing*, 39(2), 62–69. doi:10.1002/rnj.97

119. Oore, G., LeBlanc D., Day, A., Leiter, M. P., Laschinger, H. S., Price, S. L., & Latimer, M. (2010). When respect deteriorates: Incivility as a moderator of the stressor-strain relationship among hospital workers. *Journal of Nursing Management* 18, 878–888. doi:10.1111/j.1365-2834.2010.01139.x

120. Healy, S., & Tyrrell, M. (2011). Stress in emergency departments: Experiences of nurses and doctors. *Emergency Nurse*, 19(4), 31-37 doi:10.7748/en2011.07.19.4.31.c8611

121. Clark, C. (2013). National study on faculty-to-faculty incivility: Strategies to foster collegiality and civility. *Nurse Educator*, 38 (3), 98-102. doi:10.1097/NNE.0b013e31828dc1b2

122. Clark, C. M., & Springer, P. J. (2010). Academic nurse leaders' role in fostering a culture of civility in nursing education. *Journal of Nursing Education*, 49, 319-325. doi:10.3928/01484834-20100224-01

123. Simon, S., & Sauer, P. (2013). An exploration of the workplace bullying experience: Coping strategies used by nurses. Journal Nurses Profession Development 29(5), 228-232. doi:10.1097/01.NND.0000433147.33631

124. Blair, P. (2013). Lateral violence in nursing. *Journal of Emergency Nursing*, 39(5), 75-78. doi:10.1016/j.jen.2011.12.006

125. Livington, J. D., Verdun-Jones, S., Brink, J., Lussier, P., & Nicholls, T. (2013). A narrative review of the effectiveness of aggression management training programs for psychiatric hospital staff. *Journal of Forensic Nursing*, 6(1), 15–28. doi:10.1111/j.1939-3938.2009.01061.x

126. Chekwa, C., & Thomas, E. (2013). Workplace bullying: Is it a matter of growth? [Electronic version]. *Journal of Diversity Management*, 8(1), 44. Retrieved from

http://www.cluteinstitute.com/journals/journal-of-diversity-management-jdm/

127. Anthony, M., & Yastik, J. (2011). Nursing students &, experiences with incivility in clinical education. *Journal of Nursing Education*, 50, 140–144. doi:10.3928/01484834-20110131-04

128. Luparell, S. (2011). Incivility in nursing: The connection between academia and clinical settings. *Critical Care Nurse*, 31(2), 92-95. Retrieved from http://ccn.aacnjournals.org/content/31/2/92.full

129. Clarke, C. M., Kane, D. J., Rajacich, D. L., & Lafreniere, K. D. (2012). Bullying in undergraduate clinical education. *Journal of Nursing Education*, 51, 269-276. doi:10.3928/01484834-2012040 9-01

130. Marchiondo, K., Marchiondo, L. A., & Lasiter, S. (2010). Faculty incivility: Effects on program satisfaction of BSN students. *Journal of Nursing Education*, 49, 608–614. doi:10.3928/01484834-20100524-05

131. Becher, J., & Visovsky, C. (2012). Horizontal violence in nursing. *Medsurg Nursing*, 21, 210-213, 232. Retrieved from http://medsurgnursing.net/

132. Palaz, S. (2013). Turkish nursing students' perceptions and experiences of bullying behavior in nursing education. *Journal of Nursing Education and Practice*, 3(1), 23. doi:10.5430/jnep.v3n1p23

133. Wilson, B., Diedrich, A., Phelps, C., & Choi, M. (2011). Bullies at work: The impact of horizontal hostility in the hospital setting and intent to leave. *The Journal of Nursing Administration*, 41, 453-458. doi:10.1097/nna.0b013e3182346e90

134. Wilson, B. L., & Phelps, C. (2013). Horizontal hostility. *Journal of Nursing Administration Healthcare Law, Ethics and Regulation*, 15(1), 51–57. doi:10.1097/nhl.0b013e3182861503

135. Ashker, V. E., Penprase, B., & Salman, A. (2012). Work-related emotional stressors and coping strategies that affect the well-being of nurses working in hemodialysis units. *Nephrology*

REFERENCES

Nursing Journal, 39, 231-236. Retrieved from http://www.annanurse.org/nnj

136. Gibson, J. L., Ivancevich, J. M., Donnelly, J. H., Jr., & Konopaske, R. (2006). *Organizations: Behavior, Structure, Processes.* Boston, MA: McGraw-Hill.

137. Yonder-Wise, P. S. (2011). *Leading and Managing in Nursing* (5th ed.). St. Louis, MO: Mosby.

138. Quinlan, E., Robertson, S., Miller, N., & Robertson-Boersma, D. (2014). Interventions to reduce bullying in health care organizations: A scoping review. *Health Services Management Research,* 27(1-2), 33–44. doi:10.1177/0951484814547236

139. Strandmark, M., & Rahm, G. (2014). Development, implementation, and evaluation of a process to prevent and combat workplace bullying. *Scandinavian Journal of Public Health,* 42(15), 66–73. doi:10.1177/1403494814549494

140. Wenzel, J., Shaha, M., Klimmek, R., & Krumm, S. (2011). Working through grief and loss: Oncology nurses' perspectives on professional bereavement. *Oncology Nursing Forum,* 38, E272-282. doi:10.1188/11.ONF.E272-E282

141. Wright, K. (2014). Alleviating stress in the workplace: Advice for nurses. *Nursing Standard,* 28(20), 37–42. doi:10.7748/ns2014.01.28.20.37.e8391

142. Bennadi, D., & Konekeri, V. (2015). Workplace bullying: Beware! *Dental Hypotheses,* 6(2), 72. doi:10.4103/2155-8213.158480

143. Wild, J. R. L., Ferguson, H. J. M., McDermott, F. D., Hornby, S. T., & Gokani, V. J. (2015). Undermining and bullying in surgical training: A review and recommendations by the Association of Surgeons in Training. *International Journal of Surgery,* 23, S5– S9. doi:10.1016/j.ijsu.2015.09.017

144. Brinkert, R. (2011). Conflict coaching training for nurse managers: A case study of a two-hospital health system. *Journal of Nursing Management,* 19(1), 80–91. doi:10.1111/j.1365-2834.2010.01133.x

145. Washington State Department of Labor and Industries. (2012). *Workplace Violence Awareness and Prevention for Employers and Employees.* Retrieved from http://www.lni.wa.gov/IPUB/417-140-000.pdf

146. Wu, W. (2014). *A Systematic Review of Current Prevention and Intervention Programs Addressing Workplace Aggression* (Doctoral dissertation). Retrieved from ProQuest Dissertations and Theses database. (UMI No. 1567859)

147. U. S. Department of Labor Occupational Safety and Health Administration. (2004). *Guidelines for Preventing Workplace Violence for Health Care & Social Service Workers.* Retrieved from https://www.osha.gov/Publications/OSHA3148/osha3148.html

148. Abe, K., & Henly, S. (2010). Bullying among Japanese hospital nurses: Modeling responses to the revised negative acts questionnaire. *Nursing Research, 59,* 110-118. doi:10.1097/NNR.0b013e3181d1a709

149. Longo, J., & Hain, D. (2014). Bullying: A hidden threat to patient safety. *Nephrology Nursing Journal, 41*(2), 193-99.

150. Wyatt, R.M. (2013). Revisiting disruptive and inappropriate behavior: Five years after standards introduced. *Joint Commission Physician Blog.* Retrieved from http://www.jointcommission.org/jc_physician_blog/revisiting_disruptive_and_inappropriate_behavior/

152. McNamara, S. A. (2012). Incivility in nursing: unsafe nurse, unsafe patients. *Association Perioperative Registered Nurses Journal, 95,* 535–540. doi:10.1016/j.aorn.2012.01.020

153. Leon-Perez, J. M., Arenas, A., Medina, F. J., & Munduate Jaca, L. (2011). *Confront the conflict or leave it alone? The role of conflict management styles in the relationship between interpersonal conflict and workplace bullying.* International Association for Conflict Management 24th Annual Conference. doi:10.2139/ssrn.1872864

154. Appelbaum, S. H., Semerjian, G., & Mohan, K. (2012). Workplace bullying: Consequences, causes and controls (Part 1).

Industrial and Commercial Training, 44, 203-210. doi:10.1108/00197851211231478

155. Holloway, I., & Biley, F. (2011). Being a qualitative researcher. *Qualitative Health Research,* 21, 968-975. doi:10.1177/1049732310395607

156. Smith, J. A. (2011). Evaluating the contribution of interpretative phenomenological analysis. *Health Psychology Review,* 5, 9-27. doi:10.1080/17437199.2010.510659

157. Yin, R. K. (2011). *Qualitative Research from Start to Finish.* New York, NY: The Guilford Press.

158. Yin, R. K. (2014). *Case Study Research: Design and Methods* (5th ed.). Los Angeles, CA: Sage.

159. Longhofer, J., Floersch, J., & Hoy, J. (2012). *Qualitative Methods for Practice Research.* New York, NY: Oxford University Press. Retrieved from http://www.oxfordscholarship.com

160. Salkind, N. J. (2009). *Exploring Research* (7th ed.). Upper Saddle River, NJ: Prentice Hall.

161. Levine, E. (2011). Quantitative research. In *Encyclopedia of Nursing Research.* New York, NY: Springer.

162. Leech, N. L., & Onwuegbuzie, A. J. (2009). A typology of mixed methods research designs. *Quality and Quantity,* 43, 265-275. doi:10.1007/s11135-007-9105-3

163. Hoe, J., & Hoare, Z. (2012). Understanding quantitative research: Part 1. *Nursing Standard,* 27(15), 52–57. doi:10.7748/ns2012.12.27.15.52.c9485

164. Brown, R. B. (2006). *Doing your dissertation in business and management: The reality of research and writing.* Thousand Oaks, CA: Sage.

165. Hammer, C. (2011). From the editor: Expanding our knowledge base through qualitative research methods. *American Journal of Speech-Language Pathology,* 20(3), 1-2. doi:10.1044/1058-0360(2011/ed-01)

166. Ivey, J. (2013). Interpretive phenomenology. *Pediatric*

Nursing, 39(1), 27. Retrieved from http://www.journals.elseier.com/journal-of-pediatric-nursing/

167. Husserl, E. (1963/1913). Ideas: *A General Introduction to Pure Phenomenology* (W. R. Boyce Gibson, Trans.). New York, NY: Collier. (Original published 1913)

168. Oklahoma Board of Nursing. (2014). *Fiscal Year Statistics.* Retrieved from http://www.ok.gov/nursing.rnbycofld12.pdf

169. United States Census Bureau. (2014). State and county quick facts. Retrieved from http://quickfacts.census.gov/qfd/states/40000.html

170. Healthy Workplace Bill. (2014). *History of the U.S. Legislative Campaign.* Retrieved from http://www.healthyworkplacebill.org

171. Stagg, S. J., Sheridan, D. J., Jones, R. A., & Speroni, K. G. (2013). Workplace bullying: The effectiveness of a workplace program. *Workplace Health Safety,* 61, 333–338. doi:10.3928/21650799-20130716-03

172. Purpora, C., Blegen, M., & Stotts, N. (2012). Horizontal violence among hospital staff nurses related to oppressed self or oppressed group. *Journal of Professional Nursing,* 28, 306-314. doi:10.1016/j.profnurs.2012.01.001

173. Baldridge Performance Excellence Program (2015). *Baldridge Award Recipient Information.* Retrieved from http://patapsco.nist.gov/award_recipients/index.cfm

174. Behere, S., Yadav, R., & Behere, P. (2011). A comparative study of stress among students of medicine, engineering, and nursing. *Indian Journal of Psychological Medicine,* 33, 145-148. doi:10.4103/0253-7176.92064

175. Saunders, P., Huynh, A., & Goodman-Delahunty, J. (2007). Defining workplace bullying behaviors professional lay definitions of workplace bullying. *International Journal of Law and Psychiatry,* 30, 340-354. doi:10.1016/j.ijlp.2007.06.007

176. Baum, B. (2013). Human resource policies on workplace safety: A case for incorporating anti-bullying measures. *Journal of American Academy of Business*, 21(2), 40-45.

177. Van Hulle, H., & Marshall, D. (2016). Workplace bullying in nursing – Part 2: Prevention and management. *OOHNA Journal*, 35(1). Retrieved from http://addictionsunplugged.com/wp-content/uploads/2016/04/Spring-Summer-2016-OOHNA-Journal.pdf

178. Lachman, V. D. (2014). Ethical issues in the disruptive behaviors of incivility, bullying, and horizontal/lateral violence. *Medsurg Nursing*, 23(1), 56-58, 60.

179. Read, E., & Laschinger, H. K. (2013). Correlates of new graduate nurses' experiences of workplace mistreatment. JONA: *The Journal of Nursing Administration*, 43, 221–228. doi:10.1097/nna.0b013e3182895a90

180. Karatuna, I. (2015). Targets' coping with workplace bullying: A qualitative study. Qualitative Research in Organizations & Management, 10(1), 21–37. doi:10.1108/qrom-09-2013-1176

181. Managing workplace conflict. (2016). *Human Resource Management International Digest*, 24(1), 16–18. doi:10.1108/hrmid-10-2015-0157

182. Christie, W., & Jones, S. (2013). Lateral violence in n theory of the nurse as wounded healer. OLIN: *The Online Journal of Issues in Nursing*, 9(1), 1-9. doi:10.3912/OJIN.Vol19No01PPT01

183. Price, D., Green, D., Spears, B., Scrimgeour, M., Barnes, A., Geer, R., & Johnson, B. (2013). A qualitative exploration of cyber-bystanders and moral engagement. *Australian Journal of Guidance and Counseling*, 24(1), 1–17. Retrieved from doi:10.1017/jgc.2013.18

184. Bureau of Labor Statistics. (2014). *Occupational outlook handbook: Registered nurses.* Retrieved from http://www.bls.gov/ooh/healthcare/registered-nurses.htm

185. Carbo, J. (2009). Strengthening the healthy workplace act-

lessons from Title VII and IIED litigation and stories of targets' experiences. *Journal of Workplace Rights*, 14(1) 97-120.

186. Fardellone, C., & Click, E. R. (2013). Self-perceived leadership behaviors of clinical ladder nurses. *Nurse Leader*, 11(6), 51–53. doi:10.1016/j.mnl.2013.05.016

187. Miller, W. R. (2010). Qualitative research findings as evidence. *Clinical Nurse Specialist*, 24, 191–193. doi:10.1097/nur.0b013e3181e36087

188. Miller, M., & Hartung, S. Q. (2011). Covert crime at work. *Pennsylvania Nurse*, 66(4), 11-16. Retrieved from http://psna.org

189. Walrafen, N., Brewer, K., & Mulvenon, C. (2012). Sadly caught up in the moment: An exploration of horizontal violence. *Nursing Economics*, 30, 6-12, 49. Retrieved from http://www.medscape.com/viewarticle/760015

190. Riskin, A., Erez, A., Foulk, T. A., Kugelman, A., Gover, A., Shoris, I., Riskin, K., & Bamberger, P. A. (2015). The impact of rudeness on medical team performance: A randomized trial. *Pediatrics*, 136, 487–495. doi:10.1542/peds.2015-1385

191. Siegrist, J., Shackelton, R., Link, C., Marceau, L., von dem Knesebeck, O., & McKinlay, J. (2010). Work stress of primary care physicians in the US, UK, and German health care systems. *Social Science & Medicine*, 71, 298–304. doi:10.1016/j.socscimed.2010.03.043

192. Wren, J. T. (1995). *The Leader's Companion Insights on Leadership Through the Ages*. New York, NY: Free Press.

193. Happell, B., Reid-Searl, K., Dwyer, T., Caperchione, C.M., Gaskin, C.J., & Burke, K.J. (2013). *How Nurses Cope with Occupational Stress Outside Their Workplace*, Collegian, 20(3), 195-199, doe:10.1016/j.colegn.2012.08.003

Additional Resources
Abawi, L. (2012). Introducing refractive phenomenology.

International Journal of Multiple Research Approaches, 6, 141-149. doi:10.5172/mra.2012.6.2.141

Balls, P. (2009). Phenomenology in nursing research: Methodology, interviewing and transcribing. *Nursing Times*, 105(31), 30-33. Retrieved from http://www.nursingtimes.net

Barrett, J. R. (2007). The researcher as instrument: Learning to conduct qualitative research through analyzing and interpreting a choral rehearsal. *Music Education Research*, 9, 417–433. doi:10.1080/14613800701587795

Barusch, A., Gringeri, C., & George, M. (2011). Rigor in qualitative social work research: A review of strategies used in published articles. *Psychology of Sport and Exercise*, 35, 11-19. doi:10.1093/swr/35.1.11

Braun, V., & Clarke, V. (Eds.). (2012). Thematic analysis. *In APA[85] handbook of research methods in psychology: Research designs: quantitative, qualitative, neuropsychological and biological* (Vol 2, pp. 57-71). Washington, DC: American Psychological Association. doi:10.1037/13620-004

Corbin, J. A., & Strauss, A. (2008). *Basics of Qualitative Research* (3rd ed.). Thousand Oaks, CA: Sage.

Dialsingh, I. (2008). Mail survey. *Encyclopedia of Survey Research Methods.* doi:10.4135/9781412963947.n282

DiCicco-Bloom, B., & Crabtree, B. (2006). The qualitative research interview. *Medical Education*, 40, 314-321. doi:10.1111/j.1365-2929.2006.02418.x

Dillman, D. A. (1991). The design and administration of mail surveys. *Annual Review Sociology.* 17(1), 225–249. doi:10.1146/annurev.so.17.080191.001301

Dillman, D. A. (1999). *Mail and Internet Surveys: The Tailored Design Method.* (2nd ed.) New York, NY: John Wiley & Sons.

Fain, J. (2010). Should we publish pilot/feasibility studies? *The Diabetes Educator*, 36, 521-521. doi:10.1177/0145721710379355

Flood, A. (2010). Understanding phenomenology. *Nurse Researcher*, 17(2), 7-15. doi:10.7748/nr2010.01.17.2.7.c7457

REFERENCES

Francis, J., Johnston, M., Robertson, C., Glidewell, L., Entwistle, V., Eccles, M., & Grimshaw, J. (2010). What is an adequate sample size? Operationalising data saturation for theory-based interview studies. *Psychology & Health*, 25, 1229-1245. doi:10.1080/08870440903194015

Gibbs, G. R., Clarke, D., Taylor, C., Silver, C., & Lewins, A. (2015). *Welcome to Online QDA*. Retrieved from http://onlineqda.hud.ac.uk/index.php

Green, B. (2013). Narrative inquiry and nursing research. *Qualitative Research Journal*, 13(1), 62–71. doi:10.1108/14439881311314586

Guest, G., MacQueen, K. M., Namey, E. E. (2012). *Applied Thematic Analysis*. Thousand Oaks, CA: Sage.

Hardicre, J. (2014). Valid informed consent in research: An introduction. *British Journal of Nursing*, 23(11), 564–567. doi:10.12968/bjon.2014.23.11.564

Houghton, C., Casey, D., Shaw, D., & Murphy, K. (2013). Rigour in qualitative case-study research. *Nurse Researcher*, 20(4), 12-17. doi:10.7748/nr2013.03.20.4.12.e326

Lee, E., Mishna, F., & Brennenstuhl, S. (2010). How to critically evaluate case studies in social work. *Research on Social Work Practice*, 20, 682-689. doi:10.1177/1049731509347864

Liu, J., & Graves, N. (2011). Childhood bullying: A review of constructs, concepts, and nursing implications. *Public Health Nursing*, 28, 556-568. doi:10.1111/j.1525-1446.2011.00972.x

Mertens, D. M. (2005). *Research Methods in Education and Osychology: Integrating Diversity with Quantitative and Qualitative Approaches* (2nd ed.). Thousand Oaks, CA: Sage.

Miles, M. B., Huberman, A. M., & Saldaña, J. (2014). *Qualitative Data Analysis: A Methods Sourcebook* (3rd ed.). Thousand Oaks, CA: Sage.

Moon, M. D., Wolf, L. A., Baker, K., Carmen, M. J., Clark, P. R., Henderson, D., & Zavotsky, K. E. (2013). Evaluating qualitative research studies for use in the clinical setting. *Journal of Emergency Nursing, 39,* 508-510. doi:10.1016/j.jen.2013.06.009

Morgan, D. (2008). Sampling frame. In L. Given (Ed.), *The SAGE Encyclopedia of Qualitative Research Methods* (pp. 801-802). Thousand Oaks, CA: Sage. doi:10.4135/9781412963909.n414

Morin, K. (2013). Value of a pilot study. *Journal of Nursing Education, 52,* 547-548. doi:10.3928/01484834-20130920-10

Murphy, F. J., & Yielder, J. (2010). Establishing rigour in qualitative radiography research. *Radiography, 16,* 62-67. doi:10.1016/j.radi.2009.07.003

Palys, T. (2008). Purposive sampling. In L. Given (Ed.), *The SAGE Encyclopedia of Qualitative Research Methods* (pp. 698-699). Thousand Oaks, CA: Sage. doi:10.4135/9781412963909.n349

Pereira, H. R. (2012). Rigour in phenomenological research: Reflections of a novice nurse researcher. *Nurse Researcher, 19(3),* 16-19. doi:10.7748/nr2012.04.19.3.16.c9054

Pernecky, T., & Jamal, T. (2010). Hermeneutic phenomenology in tourism studies. *Annals of Tourism Research, 37,* 1055-1075. doi:10.1016/j.annals.2010.04.002

Pratt, M. (2012). The utility of human sciences in nursing inquiry. *Nurse Researcher, 19(3),* 12-15. doi:10.7748/nr2012.04.19.3.12.c9053

QSR International (2011). *What is qualitative research?* Retrieved from http://www.qsrinternational.com/what-is-qualitative-research.aspx

Radwin, L., & Cabral, H. (2010). Trust in nurses scale: Construct validity and internal reliability evaluation. *Journal of Advanced Nursing, 66,* 683-689. doi:10.1111/j.1365-2648.2009.05168.x

Randles, C. (2012). Phenomenology: A review of the literature. *Update: Applications of Research in Music Education, 30(2),* 11-21. doi:10.1177/8755123312436988

Roberts, C. M. (2010). *The Dissertation Journey: A Practical and*

Comprehensive Guide to Planning, Writing, and Defending Your Dissertation. Newbury Park, CA: Corwin Press.

Saldaña, J. (2013). *The Coding Manual for Qualitative Researchers* (2nd ed.). London: Sage.

Sayrs, L. (1998). An introduction to qualitative research interviewing. *American Journal of Evaluation*, 19, 267–270. doi:10.1177/109821409801900217

Stake, R. E. (1995). *The Art of Case Study Research.* Thousand Oaks, CA: Sage.

Suri, H. (2011). Purposeful sampling in qualitative research synthesis. *Qualitative Research Journal*, 11, 63-75. doi:10.3316/qrj1102063

Taylor, R. (2013). Case-study research in context. *Nurse Researcher*. 20(4), 4-5. Retrieved from www. nursereacher.co.uk

Thomas, E., & Magilvy, J. (2011). Qualitative rigor or research validity in qualitative research. *Journal for Specialists in Pediatric Nursing*, 16, 151-155. doi:10.1111/j.1744-6155.2011.00283.x

Tracy, S. (2010). Qualitative quality: Eight "big-tent" criteria for excellent qualitative research. *Qualitative Inquiry*, 16, 837-851. doi:10.1177/1077800410383121

Tufford, L., & Newman, P. (2012). Bracketing in qualitative research. *Qualitative Social Work*, 11(1), 80-96. doi:10.1177/1473325010368316

Walker, J. L. (2012). The use of saturation in qualitative research. *Canadian Journal of Cardiovascular Nursing*, 22(2), 37-41. Retrieved from http://journals.lww.com/jcnjournal/pages/default.aspx

ABOUT THE AUTHOR

Dr. Phyllis Browning is a nurse entrepreneur specializing in geriatric care, presently working as a regional nurse consultant. During her 17-year career in the health care sector, Dr. Browning has excelled in a wide range of roles, progressing from registered nurse to Director of Nursing and Quality Assurance Consultant in the areas of hospital and long-term care. As a part of her doctoral dissertation, she studied factors affecting nurse anti-bullying training outcomes. Her extensive experience in clinical settings and passion for her profession prompted Dr. Browning to focus her research on workplace health and safety, nurse wellness and ensuring optimum patient care.

Made in the USA
Lexington, KY
19 August 2018